How to Suffer *Well*:
Timeless Knowledge on Dealing with Hardship and Becoming Anguish-Proof

By Peter Hollins,
Author and Researcher at
petehollins.com

Table of Contents

1. To suffer is to live

There isn't a religious tradition or philosophy out there, modern or ancient, that hasn't attempted to tackle the problem of suffering. In fact, why people should experience pain and suffer at all is a fact of life that humankind has been wrestling with since... well, probably since the very first moment we suffered!

While some have attempted to explain why it happens, others have focused on dissecting it as a phenomenon, trying to either reduce it, or investigate whether pain can, to some degree, be put to good use. Some have even suggested that our resistance and wrestling with the concept of pain and adversity is itself causing us to suffer. The Buddhists tell a story that goes like this:

Long ago, there was a farmer who had problems. He was advised to go and see the Buddha, who was wise and would help him sort his life out. The Buddha asked him why he had come.

"I'm a farmer," he said. "I love farming, but the problem is that sometimes there's no rain, and we really struggle those years. Of course, sometimes we have the other problem, and there's too much rain and the floods destroy everything." But the man didn't stop there.

"I also have a wife, Buddha. I love her, truly, but sometimes we don't get on. To be honest, occasionally, she gets on my nerves. And my kids! They're lovely kids. They're great. Sometimes, though, they misbehave like you wouldn't believe..."

The farmer went on and on like this. His in-laws were bothering him, he had money worries, he'd often tossed and turned in bed at night wondering about the meaning of life, and his left knee hurt. The Buddha listened patiently, smiled, and simply said, "I can't help you."

The farmer was astonished.
The Buddha continued, "Every person has 83 problems, every one of us. And there's nothing you can do about it. Maybe you can do this or that to fix them, but once one problem is gone, another one springs up in its place. More problems are coming – for example, you will lose your family and loved ones one day, and you yourself will die. *That's* a problem you certainly can't do anything about."
The farmer, probably beginning to regret his visit, couldn't help but ask angrily, "Well, I thought you could help! What's the point of everything you teach if you can't solve my problems?"
"Well, I can maybe help you with your *eighty-fourth* problem," he said.
"Eighty-fourth problem? Well, what's that?"
"It's that you want to not have any problems."

This attitude underlies the general Buddhist perspective, which is that pain is inevitable, and it is our *clinging to* or resistance to that experience that causes us problems. In other words, if we practice non-attachment and stop fighting with reality, we can learn to live peacefully in a world that will always contain problems.

The ancient historical Buddha would have likely found our current day obsession with happiness and success and ease quite amusing. All of Buddha's four "noble truths" are in some way about suffering, not blissful, perfect happiness that frees us from the troubles of the world forever.

If you're a person living in the modern industrialized world, though, you probably view suffering quite differently from the Buddhists of thousands of years ago. You might not even believe that you do suffer – isn't suffering something that poor starving children in Africa do? You might look at your own boredom or malaise or low self-esteem as a mere mental health problem rather than call it something as dramatic as "suffering." But that's exactly how the Buddhists would characterize it.

They would call countless everyday experiences suffering: loving someone a little more than they love you, feeling uncertain about your job, getting old, looking in the mirror and not liking what you see, feeling disappointed that you didn't achieve more with your life, or quietly wondering what the point of it all is... all of this is suffering. When you're stressed out, frustrated, worried, depressed, annoyed, overwhelmed, resentful, or fearful... then you're suffering.

Call it anguish, stress, unhappiness, dissatisfaction – all of this happens because we are grasping hold of something that is by nature impermanent.

Importantly, in this worldview, suffering is everywhere and unavoidable. Since life is always changing, we will one day have to face losing what we have now. In other words, it's not possible not to suffer – illness, death, confusion, relationship breakups, and conflict are all a non-negotiable part of life. The Buddhists would say that the way forward is not to fight this fact but to work with it. The idea, then, is not that we vanquish suffering or run away from it, but rather that we find deeper meaning and understanding in the inevitable experience.

What *is* suffering? Some people would say that it is the tendency to wish that things weren't the way they are, i.e. to be like the farmer whose main problem is that he thinks he should have no problems. We can see this perspective on suffering in many different philosophies and worldviews, not just Buddhism.

Imagine you are in love with someone and announce your feelings only to have them tell you they don't see you that way. It feels awful. But *why*? Some would say that the awful feelings stem from our faulty interpretation, not from the experience itself. Maybe we have a deep, unexamined belief that we don't deserve to feel bad. That we are required in life to get what we want. More specifically, perhaps we've told ourselves that this person loving us back is a condition for our own happiness.

But is it? Is there anything in objective reality, however you define it, that suggests that your awful feelings are somehow a mistake?

We arrive again at what some would say is the root cause of suffering – our attitude. We experience reality (that is, we experience that it changes, is impermanent, and occasionally hurts) and we try to deny it. For example, we stubbornly do whatever we can to prevent ageing, and deny that we are getting older. When we lose something, or someone dies, we rail against the fact and fight it, believing it is an injustice. When luck doesn't favor us, we call it "unfair." It's all just many different ways of saying, "the way things are isn't right. They should be some other way."

Right now, try to think of all the things you believe are missing from your life: money, a relationship, a good career, and so on. Now, imagine a person who has this thing you want. Look at them and ask yourself honestly, is their life genuinely any better than yours? Are they spared any suffering that you aren't? Are they completely immune from disappointment and bad days and feeling ungrateful? Truth is, even though they have the thing you want, they too will have to say goodbye to it at some point.

To summarize this perspective on suffering, we can put it this way: **pain is inevitable, suffering is not.**

What's the difference between pain and suffering? Aren't they the same thing?

Imagine you are stung by a bee. It's completely unexpected, and the pain quickly fills your body, bringing tears to your eyes. In a flash, you're angry – stupid bee! What's the point of a bee stinging you like that, for no reason? And then it dies anyway? You start shouting and yelling, cursing your luck, and wondering what you did to deserve such a random bit of agony to come your way. You're in a bad mood the rest of the day, even snapping at someone who asks if it's still hurting.

Let's pick it apart. The bee sting? That was just life. Bees exist, humans exist, and occasionally a bee will sting someone. Today that someone was you. You're a flesh-and-blood body that can get damaged, so when a bee stings you, it hurts like hell. So far, so good. We are looking at what the Buddhists would call reality. Life is impermanent, things change, and sometimes it hurts. We are in the realm of **pain**. In fact, your body cannot help but automatically respond to pain – tears in your eyes, redness and swelling on the skin.

But that's not all there is in the story. There is also the big, complicated story you tell about the pain – it's unfair, stupid, why did it have to happen, etc. The anger you feel is not a direct result of the bee's stinger entering our flesh. You are the source of that anger, or more accurately, the stories you tell about that bee sting cause the anger. Long after the pain has faded, you're still in a bad mood. You snap at someone. You are now well in the realms of **suffering**.

If you are alive, you will experience pain. This is inevitable. No escape.
But we do have a choice about how much we suffer.

The facts of life are what they are, but our experience is heavily determined by how we respond to and interpret those facts. So, we can see that there are two ways to understand and deal with the fact that bad things happen to us:

1. Try to eradicate pain itself
2. Try to change our perception of that pain

The Buddhists would say that number 1 creates more suffering since eradicating pain is a metaphysical impossibility. You'll exhaust yourself just as surely as you would trying to argue away mountains or the sea. They exist, whether we like it or not. Number 2 doesn't remove the pain, but it does remove the source of the suffering – us.

We'll see some version of this big idea in several different forms throughout this book. The early Buddhists understood something powerful: that as much as we don't like it, there really isn't anything we can do about the pain in life. That leaves us to control what we can – our relationship to it, our perception of it, as well as our behavior and belief.

Ideas like, "the world is unfair and has victimized me" or "I don't deserve this" actually have no basis in reality. They come from within us. These beliefs lead to depression and anxiety and a world of problems – not the pain itself.

Of course, proponents of this worldview would say that just because pain is inevitable, it doesn't mean we are doomed to sit down and take whatever life throws at us. We can take action, solve problems, set goals for ourselves and achieve them. However, you might notice that none of this constructive action requires us to suffer. In other words, suffering doesn't actually help.

Pain is just pain. It comes, it goes.
But pain plus our resistance equals suffering. And this can go on forever if we want it to!

Buddhists and psychologists alike talk about the power of "sitting with" an emotion rather than going to war with it, trying to run away from it, or clinging to it in the fear it will disappear (hint: it will!). Though it might seem like a defeatist attitude on the surface, accepting and acknowledging pain actually means you're able to let it pass (hint: it also will!). The burn of the bee sting will fade, your hurt and surprise will dissipate, and the pain of unrequited love will diminish in time.

This particular take on suffering is not the only perspective, though. In the much-loved book *Man's Search for Meaning*, Viktor Frankl writes convincingly about his understanding of suffering and how we can make sense of it. And he should know – being a prisoner in the Nazi concentration camps, he lived while his parents, brother and pregnant wife were all killed.

Pain is one thing, but Frankl describes something most of us can truly not conceive of. He had *everything* stripped from him. In fact, this was what inspired him to write so passionately about what they couldn't take away – his dignity. His ability to choose his response to events that he did not choose. His conscious will and the decisions he would make about what his experience meant to him.

He says it succinctly: "Between stimulus and response there is a space. In that space is our power to choose our response. In our response lies our growth and our freedom." As a matter of urgency, Frankl discovered his own psycho-spiritual authority, his own strength, and his own power. We'll look at Frankl's perceptive in more detail in a later chapter. For now, basically, his life was evidence that growth and evolution were possible, even despite an unspeakable of adversity, distress and deprivation.

So, he talks about it in terms of stimulus and response. The pain is a stimulus, but what will our response be?

Pain is a purely physiological response. Your body has evolved sophisticated mechanisms to keep it safe, and that typically involves an involuntary neurochemical response. But, Frankl talks about that "little space" beyond what is automatic. When we are aware, we can decide what we will do next. We choose whether that pain completely destroys us, or whether it catalyzes a deeper transformation in us. We decide whether we're going to grab hold of annoyance or outrage or disappointment, or whether we're going to move on and focus our attention elsewhere. We can decide to blame or forgive. We can decide what stories we want to tell about what has happened to us, and why.

What Frankl brought to the discussion of suffering was the question of recovery. We can endure, tolerate and accommodate adversity. But what if we could also grow from it, and be stronger and better than before? What if crisis and pain were an opportunity to learn?

Those inspired by Frankl's writings took a very empowering and dignified approach to the fact of pain. They looked at things like anxiety, guilt, shame, depression, hopelessness, loneliness and existential suffering, and saw that much of it came down to the meaning we ascribed to experiences. Our beliefs, our mindset, our personal myths and narratives – all of these things allow one person to see a catastrophe as a new beginning, and another as a complete failure.

So, rather than asking what suffering is, we can also ask *where* it is. The Nazi captors who imprisoned and tortured people in concentration camps undoubtedly inflicted incredible pain on those people. But in truth, the prisoners themselves took that pain and did very many different things with it. Some collapsed and gave up hope. Some were defiant. Some deliberately chose to believe in the goodness of human beings, forcefully asserting their will to something greater, despite the atrocities around them.

So, is the suffering out there or in here, within us?

If we are depressed, what portion of our experience comes from events outside of our control, and what portion is explained by our expectations, interpretations, self-talk, narratives, beliefs and biases?

Today, cognitive behavioral therapists will say the process goes a little something like this:

- We experience pain (for example: we fail an important exam)
- In that brief moment afterwards, we begin to have negative thoughts or entertain beliefs and assumptions about this pain we experienced (maybe we think, "I'm an idiot" or we start to blame ourselves for not studying harder).
- These thoughts then lead to feelings (like shame, anxiety and self-doubt). They may also, at the same time, lead to physiological changes in our bodies (higher cortisol levels, muscle stiffness).
- These feelings and sensations then feed on themselves and spiral out of control (you feel bad about feeling bad, and so on and so on).
- In time, these thoughts and feelings may even start to manifest as behaviors and actions that further deepen your suffering (you give up studying and don't bother on the next exam, either).

The thinking goes, however, that if we are aware of the above process and can consciously step in to change it, we can go a long way to reducing suffering – basically, anything that happens after the second bullet point!

In this way, this perspective is similar to the Buddhist approach in that suffering is not dealt with directly but indirectly. We reduce the problem of suffering by addressing how we respond to inevitable pain. We are not in charge of the pain, but we are in charge of how we deal with it. This book considers countless different approaches, tactics, and techniques for making suffering work for us. But you'll notice that, even though they come from vastly different theoretical underpinnings, they each acknowledge that we are never really able to remove pain from life completely. In fact, trying to do so will likely win us more suffering, not less!

We might find this basic premise echoed in many different philosophies and ideas around suffering, including the now increasingly popular ancient school of the Stoics. Thinkers like Marcus Aurelius and

Seneca have offered their version of a healthy, constructive approach to the inevitability of pain in life. Their view can be nicely encapsulated in the famous "serenity prayer" which says, "God, grant me the serenity to accept the things I cannot change, the courage to change the things I cannot accept and the wisdom to know the difference."

They, too, understood that the good life is one that is lived with a healthy and realistic attitude towards external limitations that we have no control over. While they acknowledge that there is also scope for action, and we can always take personal responsibility for our lives, we need to understand what we can influence and what we must simply learn to live with, accept or embrace. As with the other theories we've considered here, life is improved not because suffering and pain are eradicated but because we become better at understanding, accepting and overcoming it.

Summary:

- There are countless theoretical approaches to understanding the universal problem of suffering. We start with the Buddhist conception, which sees pain as an inevitable and natural part of life, which is transient and always changing. Therefore if we attach to what is impermeant, we will suffer when it changes.
- The parable of the farmer and the Buddha shows that our biggest problem is that we believe we should have no problems.
- In these views, suffering occurs because, paradoxically, we think we should not be suffering!
- Pain is unavoidable, but suffering is optional. Suffering is pain plus our grasping, resistance, attachment or identification. Thus we can greatly reduce our suffering by changing how we deal with pain.
- The serenity prayer teaches us that we need the wisdom to discern between what is in our power to control (our mental reaction to pain) and what isn't (the pain itself).

- According to Viktor Frankl, in the brief moment after pain, we have a gap where we can pause and decide what response we would like to have. We may evolve mechanisms to respond automatically, but we also have the power to choose our response if we are conscious.
- Cognitive behavioral psychologists recognize a similar principle, and explain how our minds can trap us in suffering. We experience pain and then immediately create a thought about it. This thought creates our feelings and a physiological reaction, for example, stress and tension in the body. In time, these feelings spiral out of control and manifest as behaviors that reinforce our original thoughts.

2. Attachment is our mortal enemy

Let's dig a little deeper. Though the Buddhists had a lot to say about suffering, and though we'll return to their conception of the problem again and again, in truth, their perspective is not especially unique. What is great about the Buddhist approach is that it has a clear and defined explanation for why we suffer, i.e. where it comes from. It's a little like understanding the etiology of a disease, in this case, the disease broadly being the "human condition." We start here because once we know *why* we suffer, we're arguably better prepared to do something smart about it.

The Buddha put forward his four noble truths, which go like this:

1. Dukkha – suffering exists and is an unavoidable fact of life (at least, in this realm of existence!)
2. Samudaya – there is a cause for this suffering, which is desire, craving or attachment
3. Nirodha – we can let go of suffering by renouncing our attachment
4. Marga – we can do this by following the Buddhist "eight-fold path"

Though we will not dwell on the philosophical details too much, it's enough for now to understand the noble truths in this way: suffering happens, and it happens because we are attached to what is transient. Though, there is a solution: we can let go of suffering if we relinquish this attachment.

So, it is the nature of reality to change. When we cling and form attachments, we are in opposition to this natural order, and *this* causes us to suffer. To be released from this suffering is not to eradicate the change inherent in reality, but to cease our attachment to it.

An example will explain. Imagine you are out walking in the woods one day, and it's beautiful. It's warm and bright, the birds are singing, and you're having an amazing chat with your walking companion. It's like paradise. But it doesn't' *stay* paradise. Life always changes, and so too does this day. Maybe clouds roll in, and it starts to drizzle. The bird song stops, and your walking companion suddenly becomes grumpy and uninteresting. Suddenly, there's an annoying car alarm in the distance that goes on and on and on. Just like that, your lovely walk is not so lovely anymore.

But if we are attached to one expression of reality over another, we might tell a story that goes, "this is a problem now. It's *supposed* to be sunny and nice, and it's not." The truth is, rain and shine both belong to the natural order. Sometimes birds sing, sometimes they don't. The people we love today may be annoying and difficult tomorrow. So, we have the first noble truth – there is dukkha, or suffering. And the second noble truth is that the cause of this is you – or more accurately, it's your clinging and attachment.

For the Buddhists, nothing is permanent. Everything living will die, clouds come and go, things shift and change and evolve. Everything is always moving. However, if we cling and form attachments, we grasp hold of something and behave as though this weren't the case. We say, "I wish this day would last forever." It won't last forever, and expecting and wanting it to is what causes the pain, *not* the fact that it changes.

The four noble truth says that suffering is reduced when we let go of attachment. For example, you look up and see the drizzle and accept it. You see that your companion is grumpy, and you hear the car alarm and realize that there's nothing innately better or worse in it when compared to bird song. You don't push against it, and you don't grab hold of it, you simply say "ok" and accept the fact that, well, it *is*. And just like that, you are not suffering anymore.

When we hear the term "desire" or "attachment", we need to remember that this actually covers every instance of us wanting reality to be something that it isn't.

Every time we have an expectation for what should be, or a demand on reality, that is a desire. That is a *wanting* inside us. Whether that takes the form of greed, lust, avoidance, fascination, hope, despair or anything else, it is essentially us wanting to control reality, and make it behave in the way we think it ought to. It is this orientation to reality that causes suffering, rather than reality itself.

It's as though the eternally changing nature of life is a flowing river, and we are fallen tree branches in that river. When we align ourselves *with* the flow and position lengthwise, the river flows easily past us, and there is no issue. But when we position ourselves *against* that flow, and when we lay at right angles and resist it, there is suddenly friction. This friction is akin to suffering.

Imagine a person who stands outside in the rain and shakes their fist at the sky, yelling, "This is wrong! It's not supposed to be like this!" You'd probably find such a person faintly ridiculous, but in truth, we do the same thing all the time in life. We are always attached to what we think *should* be the case, which brings us into friction with what *is* the case. We have expectations, as though life should arrange itself according to the whims and preferences of our ego.

Why do we have expectations of life? Well, because we tell ourselves stories about the way things are. We say, "I can only be happy if things are such and so." Take a look at each of the following examples and see how the cause of suffering is not the event or situation itself, but rather the expectation that reality should have been something else:

- Someone disagrees with you on an important topic, and you're outraged by their stupidity.
- You get treated rudely by a colleague at work and feel really upset and hurt.
- The old lady in front of you in the supermarket is walking really, really slowly, and you want to pull your hair out in frustration.

Let's look closely at why you feel this way:

- You have the expectation that there is no disagreement or conflict in the world, and that others should agree with the wisdom of your opinion, or at least come around after you explain things so clearly to them!
- You hold the belief that everyone deserves respect, and that you don't deserve to be treated poorly.
- You expect everyone else to be like you, and if you are walking at a certain pace, they should walk at that pace too, and not get in your way.

Can you see how this is not all that different from standing out in the rain and yelling, "this isn't right!"?

The suffering lies in the gap between what you demand, expect or desire, and what actually is. The easiest way to see this is to imagine things from someone else's view – someone who doesn't have the same expectations as you do. Imagine that the person you're arguing with is exasperated with you and cannot imagine why *you're* so stupid. Imagine that the person criticizing you sincerely believes that you should not be doing what you're doing, and that they have to fix the situation by pointing out why you're wrong. Or picture that the old lady looks at you, shakes her head and thinks, "these people who rush around supermarkets make me want to pull my hair out in frustration!"

The fact of reality sits there, as it is. But it is *us*, and our ego and expectations, that makes up stories about what that reality is, what it should be, and what we think about it. Arguably, this is precisely why there is conflict in the world – our expectations not only fail to align with reality, but they also fail to align with other people's expectations.

We suffer because we are like little children who pout and cry because we cannot have ice cream for dinner. We fail to see the bigger picture, and we only look at events according to our own very narrow, very uninformed vision of the world. We sit and sulk, and declare that broccoli is disgusting, and that we shouldn't have to eat it. But even as adults, we can continue to do this – rating and judging reality according to the whims of our ego in the moment.

But do we *really* know what's best? Do we honestly have enough knowledge and understanding of the universal mechanisms we live within to proudly say what should and shouldn't be? It's as though we have unconsciously declared ourselves the CEOs of the universe, and are incensed when life happens without our permission, and in ways that we don't approve of.

What we have in life is a series of unfolding moments. A never-ending, ever-unfolding *now*. It's always changing. Sunshine turns to rain… turns to sunshine again. In the middle of that is us, and what we want. If we had planned a day at the beach, we would say that sunshine is good, and rain is bad. If we are gardeners or farmers, we say that rain is good and sunshine is bad. These perspectives on reality, however, are not reality itself. Rain is not good or bad, sunshine is not good or bad. It is us and our ego, our expectation and our desire to control that assigns labels to neutral reality, which is always just being what it is.

So, let's cut to the chase: what's the cause of suffering? We are.

But here, we are faced with something quite tricky. The fact is, we are individual people with unique interests and goals. We only have our own limited perspective, and of course we have a preference for all those things that favor us. This is, after all, what it means to be alive. We are not enlightened, egoless beings. We are not angels or abstract entities. We are imperfect people, living in an imperfect world.

Importantly, the Buddhists (and generally, those who teach mindfulness and awareness) don't want us to abandon all expectations. It's not possible. The idea is not to become completely apathetic, shrugging your shoulders and having no opinion about the outcome of events. It is not possible to avoid having a point of view, a judgment, or a goal. It is not possible to avoid being impacted by events around us. In other words, there will always be people we disagree with, insults, and things that get in our way.

But, we can have awareness and acceptance. We will explore the way out of suffering in more detail in the following chapter. But for now, it's important to note that we are not asked to pretend that nothing bothers us, or that we don't care what happens, either way. This is just more clinging, more ego and more expectation ("I should be more accepting" or "a truly enlightened person does such-and-such, so I must do that too...").

For now, let's acknowledge and understand the cause of suffering – that's half the problem.

Suffering *does* happen, and it happens because of our attachment.

We can call this attachment many different things: desire, craving, clinging to, positioning, searching, wanting, seeking, needing, thirsting or hungering for, resisting, obsessing about, being addicted to, grasping, identifying with, needing... Whether big or small, or profound or trivial, and whatever the object, this attachment is our active relationship to neutral reality. According to our identities, it is the personal narrative we tell about impersonal events. It is like a *contraction* – we interpret events, which requires a certain narrowing of perception.

But this is not the full story. We can also attach to and identify with neutral, fleeting events when we *push against* reality. It seems counterintuitive, but resistance is also a way of holding onto things, and failing to appreciate their transience and impermanence. For example, we can tell ourselves a complex story about our enemies or adversaries, and how much we hate them. We can get carried away with anger and blame for something that happened to us. Or, we can constantly position ourselves in opposition to something else, either because we see ourselves as victims, or perhaps as rebels, who gain our identity from what we aren't. Or consider the person who cannot even acknowledge the deep, unconscious beliefs that nevertheless control their every move. They resist these ideas to such an extent that they don't even know they're there, but their resistance and avoidance nevertheless colors everything in their life.

A Buddhist parable tells of a young monk and his wise older teacher on a journey. The pair arrive at a river and encounter a young woman having trouble crossing. The teacher thinks nothing of inviting the woman to jump on his back so he can help her cross over. The young monk, seeing this, is disturbed. He knows that in their religious tradition, touching a woman is forbidden. They continue on the journey for some time before the young monk, unable to remain silent, speaks up.

"Master, I am deeply troubled. You carried that woman across the river, but you know that this is completely against our faith."
The master smiled and simply said, "Well, I carried that woman across the river, but then I set her down again. Why have *you* been carrying her for the last three hours?"

This story shows us how clinging to and resisting are really two sides of the same coin. The young monk is both resisting reality (his master should not have carried the woman) but he is also clinging (it should be this way, not that way). Here, clinging and resisting are really different manifestations of identifying with something, to such an extent that we keep "carrying" it with us long after the fleeting event has passed.

Existence is impermanent. But when we cling or attach, we hold onto things long after they fade away. It is our stories about things that keep them alive. The master in the story above is in the moment and can let the past go. It is the young monk who suffers, because he clings and resists – he is privileging his expectation about reality above what is actually happening. The master might pause and draw the young monk's attention to the moment they are actually in. Where is the problem? Nowhere. It is only in the mind of the young monk.

We don't need to beat ourselves up about any of this. Human beings have evolved brains that seek out patterns, and try to make theories and models of the world to control whatever emerges in the present moment. Your brain evolved to help you survive – not to make you happy. Its job is to look for problems – which is not necessarily a problem in itself. However, it would help to notice how seldom this need for control actually succeeds in getting reality to behave as we wish (here's a clue: it never does). This is because life is changeable and ungraspable. Like water, in the very same instant we reach out to try and grab it, it has already flowed past. Even if we could grab hold of a moment right now, there is another one immediately on its tail, and the previous one whizzes by, never to be seen again.

Our perception, it would seem, is always colored by our interpretation and judgment. We cannot hear a sound or see a sight without deciding whether we find it pleasant or unpleasant. We cannot help but insist that if something good is happening, that it should stay that way forever, and never change. So, we build up our egos and stories and routines and rituals. Then when life smashes them to bits, we suffer.

There is a more practical way to look at the first noble truth, and that is the profound fact of, well, "shit happens." We will all die. Many, if not most of us, will experience injury and illness. If we are in a relationship, one of two things *will* happen: we will either break up, or one of us will die. You will sometimes have an accident. You will hurt yourself or hurt others. You will have something that you love and cherish, that you will nevertheless lose. If you are lucky, you will grow old and experience the indignities of an ageing body. There will be storms and unexpected bills and arguments and nasty surprises...

Seeing as these things will happen... what is the use in arguing with them?

On the other hand, even the best experiences in life are transient. No matter what peaks of pleasure you attain, they eventually stop, right? Even that delicious cookie you're eating right now will, in a minute, be no more. Then what?

The good comes and goes, and the bad comes and goes. *Everything* is transient.

But the idea is that suffering enters the picture when we strenuously try to hold onto the good, and run away from the bad. There are different types of craving and attachment. We might crave pleasure (for example, we have a food addiction), or we might cling to an ego-driven idea of our own identity (for example, we become self-obsessed and seek fame or to dominate others), or we could work hard to avoid experiencing things we don't want to experience (for example avoiding conflict, being in denial or indulging in escapism). They all amount to the same thing, though: a faulty relationship with reality. Tough, because it's hard to swallow, even the suffering attached to life's greatest losses (death, divorce etc.) are a result of our failure to accept the impermanence of everything.

Our clinging and craving are endless, and never satisfied. Unlike reality which shifts and changes, our attachment can keep going forever, going round in circles. Our seeking could turn into greed and materialism, and we find that no matter how much we have, we want more. Or our vanity causes us to build a bigger and bigger ego for ourselves. We can even find that our spiritual seeking becomes a kind of bottomless ambition, and we end up craving endless enlightenment experiences...

Summary:

- In the Buddhist tradition, the four noble truths explain what suffering is, its cause, and how to deal with it. The first truth is that suffering exists and is unavoidable, and the second is that the cause of suffering is our desire, craving or attachment. The third is that suffering can be released if we renounce this attachment, and the fourth truth is that we practice this way of being by following the eight-fold path.
- When we are attached to one outcome or another, the Buddhists claim we cause suffering. It is our perspective, preference, narrative, and expectation about what should be that causes our unhappiness. In life, everything is transient, though, and always changing.
- In the parable of the two monks, we see that resistance is also a form of grasping, and allows us to "carry" suffering with us long after the initial moment has passed.
- In this philosophy, we cannot achieve happiness by trying to remove suffering

from life, but rather by changing our attitude to it.

- We can use the four noble truths as a starting point for reducing suffering in our own lives, or rather, learn to suffer better. To do so, we have to understand our own tendency to identify with, cling, resist or tell stories about reality and learn to simply appreciate reality for what it is: neutral and impermanent.

3. How do we overcome?

In exploring the causes of suffering, we are already beginning to sketch out some possible ways to overcome it – at least according to Buddhist tradition. We look to the second and third noble truth, and see that because the cause of suffering is attachment, we can let go of suffering by letting go of attachment. Simple, right?

In theory, anyway! Finding a way to genuinely release our attachments and desires is, according to most practitioners, a life's work. We are conditioned by our culture, we are shaped by our early childhood experiences, and we are all innately primed to grasp, want and cling, rather than to flow and accept reality for what it is. *Everyone* suffers, and it's no mean feat to tackle that directly.

Think about your life right now. What form does suffering take for you?

Perhaps you are depressed or anxious, or you have relationship troubles. Maybe you struggle at work or with finances, maybe you have an addiction, or maybe your problems seem vast, abstract and difficult to pin down. Maybe the main form your suffering takes is that you're confused about what's wrong in the first place! You just know you feel bad, but you can't say why, or identify a clear path out of the trouble.

Exercise 1: Distinguishing between pain and suffering

Let's begin by simplifying things. The different shapes that suffering can take are truly endless – there might be layer upon layer of suffering, and suffering can feel like a knot made of other knots. How do you even begin to untie it all?

A great first step to help you find clarity and hopefully a sense of calm is to tease apart what is pain, and what is suffering. The Buddhist story of "the second dart" explains this difference clearly. The unavoidable pains in life are called first darts – because they are like an arrow someone shoots at us. These hurt. However, the second darts are our thoughts, reactions, and responses to the first darts. "That's so unfair!" It is like we shoot ourselves *again*, with another arrow: no longer pain, but suffering.

If we want to start identifying our role in maintaining pain, i.e. suffering, we can start by noting the difference between pain and suffering. One way to do this is to *slow everything right down,* so you can look closely at the cascade of thoughts, feelings and behaviors that occur after a painful experience.

What can happen is that, in our attempt to improve our lives, feel better or "fix" things, we focus on the second darts. We get carried away with the stories we tell ... and only end up creating even more confusion, and second and third and fourth darts. Instead, it helps to just pause and look at what is actually concrete fact out there in the world, and what is happening inside us, i.e. what exists only as interpretation, expectation, ego or narrative.

The next time you find yourself unhappy or suffering, stop. Become aware and get out a journal to help you tease things apart. First, just become aware of what is happening to you without judgment. For example, you may have just had an upsetting argument with a friend, and so you sit down with your journal. To do a "dump" of everything that is in your heart and mind, you write down the following:

I feel really angry
I don't know if I want to be his friend anymore
He thinks he's so much smarter than everyone, and I'm sick of it
I thought we were friends
Why is this happening? What have I done for him to start acting like this?
He told me I'm an idiot, but I think he's an idiot

And on and on. Without trying to judge or interpret, you just write down what is in your heart and mind. Then, when you feel you've captured the gist of it, stop and take a look at what you've written. Now, draw two columns on a piece of paper, one labelled "first darts" and the other "second darts."

Spend the next ten or twenty minutes deciding which column to place each of your thoughts, feelings and beliefs. This may take some care. You want to identify which part of your experience is a simple fact of life, part of reality and an unavoidable truth, and which part is coming from you – i.e. your attachment. It may be easier at first to simply imagine you are sifting through "fact" versus "opinion." Imagine a completely neutral third party was writing a bland news article about the situation – what would they say was pure fact?

For example, let's take the statement, "He's wrong to play the victim when *he's* the one who's being a bully." This may be a sincerely held feeling, but in truth, it's not an objective part of reality. Rather, it's a belief and interpretation that comes from your perspective. It's definitely a second dart! Likewise, "he's an idiot" is an opinion whereas, "he told me I'm an idiot" is plain fact. "He shouldn't have said that" is a second dart – and likely something that is causing more suffering than the pain of the first dart.

Sometimes, certain statements of thought and feeling hint at deeper underlying expectations. For example, "I thought we were friends" suggests a deeper expectation, i.e. "we used to be friends, and I was expecting that we would always be friends." Again, this is a second dart. It is our desire for an outcome for the situation, rather than the situation itself.

If you look at the above list, it may start to become clear just how little is fact, or a first dart. If you remove expectation, interpretation and attachment, you might be left with very little indeed: "My friend and I argued, he called me an idiot, and we may not continue to be friends." It may take you some time to pick apart situations in this way, at least at first. Often, things get confusing because we mix up facts and opinions. But though it takes time, it's worth un-mixing these things and just looking at what *is* on one side, and what our *reaction* is on the other side.

Once you do this, you will start to gain a certain clarity. When you feel like you've thoroughly dissected the situation, ask yourself the following questions:

What is the reality of my situation right now? What are the facts?
In what ways am I adding second darts to the situation?
In this situation, what is pain and what is suffering?
What can I control here, and what is out of my control?
What beliefs, expectations, and interpretations are extending or adding to the pain right now?

Here's another, simpler example. You notice you have a headache and feel miserable. You stop and ask, what is pain, and what is suffering? You realize that your head literally hurts right now, but that your mind is also filled with a whole slew of thoughts along the lines of, "this couldn't have come at a worse time, I'm so busy today!" and "I had too much coffee, that'll serve me right. I really have to fix up my lifestyle" or "I wonder if it's brain cancer..."

By simply doing this, you separate out what is pain and what is suffering, what is under your control and what isn't. Then, you give yourself the option to choose. You can take a painkiller or sit somewhere quietly while you wait for the inevitable pain of the headache to pass – which it will. And maybe, since it's entirely unnecessary, you decide not to get carried away with self-talk about the headache, which only makes things worse. You have a headache, you accept that you do... and somehow, the problem is much, much smaller.

Knowing how to discern between fact and opinion, or between first and second darts, won't make all your problems disappear. But it *will* stop you from making them bigger than they have to be, or holding onto them long after they have naturally moved on.

Exercise 2: Finding the middle way

By now, you're probably beginning to better understand the title of this book: how to suffer *well*. That we will suffer is a given. But we can choose to master this inevitable fact of life, even making an art of it. Sadly, many popular Buddhist ideas have trickled into the Western mainstream, but not before getting a little mangled in the process.

When we pass certain Buddhist concepts through our pre-existing framework, we can sometimes land up with beliefs that are rather limiting: for example, the unconscious belief that if we meditate enough, if we are mindful enough, if we are detached and spiritual and pure enough, then somehow, we won't have to suffer. We may secretly hope that we can attain nirvana and never have to suffer again.

We may feel that if we are unhappy, we are doing something wrong. It's a black and white, all-or-nothing view: either we are in blissful happiness and perfection, or we are bad and wrong. It sounds extreme, but how many self-help books out there are covertly promising exactly that?

But light and dark go together. Happiness can be grasped because it occurs alongside sadness. In our world of polarity, opposites are not at war with one another – they are mutually defining. Thus, our wellbeing and peace necessarily exists with and because of our confusion and anxiety. We cannot reach a state of no-suffering any more than we can find a mountain that only has a downhill, and not an uphill. As Thich Nhat Hanh says, no mud, no lotus. When we see the world in such a black and white way – and value only one binary – then we are not seeing reality as it is. And we invite more suffering.

Many psychologists call this particular way of thinking a cognitive distortion, and cognitive behavioral therapists work hard to empower people to notice when they're doing it – so they can choose something else. If you are suffering, pause and become aware of what is going on inside you. Try to seek the "middle path" and avoid extremes, and see if you're engaging in all-or-nothing thinking. For example:

"This entire situation is hopeless."
"This kind of thing always happens."

"I will never get to the bottom of this."
"I am a failure."
"You can't trust anybody."
"I have no choice here. It's this crummy job or I don't eat."

There is a harshness and inflexibility in all of these statements that actually doesn't reflect reality. When we see absolute terms like *always*, *never*, *everyone*, *nothing*, *completely* and so on, we know we are likely in a polarized, black-and-white mindset. But look at nature: it's complex, soft, dynamic, and plays out in endless grey areas subject to constant change.

Black-and-white thinking can be thought of as a kind of grasping or attachment – it's like looking at a single frame of a movie and making a pronouncement about the *entire* movie based on that tiny moment. If we look at one event, one thought, or one action and make a definitive statement about everything everywhere, we are no longer in the moment, and we are no longer perceiving reality. We are telling ourselves a story – and the difference between that story and what is actually happening will often be a source of suffering.

In the Buddhist tradition, the middle path is the one we take when we avoid extremes. There is no absolute position but rather a constant flow along with the ever-changing moment. You do not have to be a brilliant and perfect angelic being, and not being so does not mean you are a repugnant waste of space, either! You don't have to starve yourself, but it's probably best not to binge, either. The middle way is not just about moderation, though, it's a metaphysical position: when we adopt the middle way, we are more aligned with life itself and at peace with the nature of reality, which is impermanent and illusory. Truthfully, extremism is often something that stems from our ego's need for control and certainty, rather than from our direct perception of life around us.

To reduce your own suffering and practice more nuanced thinking, be on the lookout for exaggerations, generalizations and assumptions. Be aware of any time you are making a blanket statement based on very little information – or none at all. Then, look to see if you can soften or moderate them. Let's take a closer look, considering our earlier examples:

"This kind of thing always happens."

Does it really **always** happen? Every single time, in the history of everything? Probably not. By telling yourself that this is a permanent state of affairs, you increase your resentment, powerlessness and anger at the situation. You especially stop yourself from imagining or discovering a potential solution. Instead, you could remove that absolute word "always" and soften it to "sometimes." Isn't that more comfortable? You could even go a step further: "this kind of thing is happening right now." There is instantly more light and more ease. You acknowledge the pain, without adding on extra suffering by imagining that the pain is eternal.

"I will never get to the bottom of this."

Again, will you never? Ever? If you can instead say, "I haven't gotten to the bottom of this yet" you are creating less suffering for yourself. You are looking at the moment, as it is, rather than inviting anxiety and needless suffering by making definitive pronouncements about what hasn't even happened yet.

"I am a failure."

While there are no absolute terms here, the statement is still a cognitive distortion – failure is something that happens, it isn't what people *are*. We will suffer if we think this not only because it's a harsh thought, but because we will be prolonging a temporary situation (failing) by believing that it says something about our lasting character as people. We could instead say, "I failed" or even "I didn't succeed." Even better, we could say nothing, and simply carry on trying to achieve what we were in the first place!

"You can't trust anybody."

It doesn't take long to see how black-and-white this is. The kind of cognitive distortion we see here is called overgeneralization. One person hurts us, and that means that all people will hurt us. Which is more painful, knowing that one person hurt you, or that every single living soul also has the potential to hurt you? Thinking about it, this belief may do more damage than any single person ever could!

"I have no choice here. It's this crummy job or I don't eat."

Whenever you find yourself narrowing the entire realm of possibility down to just two options, you are, by definition, in all or nothing thinking. You are artificially setting up a trap for yourself, and deliberately shutting out other perspectives. When you indulge in either/or thinking, you suffer. But this is unnecessary suffering. You can also choose to frame it as both/and – or abandon the binary completely! When someone says, "you're with me or you're against me" they are creating a conflict where none might exist. They're creating suffering. Instead, get curious. What options do you have? When you pit two options against one another, are they really so different? Maybe when you told yourself that it was Team A vs. Team B, you missed the fact that *both* could win.

To find the middle way, prick your ears for any time you are speaking in absolutes, or using black-and-white thinking. Then try to find the moderate path between both these extremes. At the very least, there is a lot of relief and serenity to be found sometimes in simply saying, "I don't know."

Exercise 3: Embrace what is

It's a mistake to think that to be happy, we need to get rid of all suffering within us. We need to smooth over all difficulties, solve all problems and redeem all our bad traits and weaknesses. But this is just more black and white thinking – "either I'm happy, or I'm sad." A mindset shift comes when we realize that we can, in fact, live good lives *and* suffer. We don't have to wait for everything to be perfect and painless – we can be content and well, right now, with everything just as it is.

This is perhaps the most difficult task in the modern world, designed at every turn to distract us. We are constantly bombarded with ads trying to sell us solutions, with addictions promising to numb out our pains, with entertainment to soothe our sense of malaise, and noise and confusion around every corner. The unspoken message is always: happiness is elsewhere. First, you must buy this product, read this book, or achieve this goal. You must be this person before you are worthy of being happy.

Really, the message goes deeper than this: *whatever you do, escape the present moment, which is difficult and flawed and uncomfortable. Instead, flee to the past or the future, or some hypothetical fantasy world.*

But that is not where we find peace or happiness! The irony is that so much of our suffering comes not from reality itself, and the pain that naturally occurs because of its impermanence but from our constant desire to flee that reality. To run away from what is. Instead of sitting in the moment and allowing it to unfold as it is, our minds run around at a thousand miles an hour. We imagine what *might* happen, and stress about what has already happened – and long gone.

Because we are afraid of pain, we suffer more. Because we don't know how to deal with suffering, how to suffer *well*, we do it badly, and end up suffering more, and for longer than is "necessary." If we know how to suffer, we suffer less. If we don't fear suffering, we don't push against it and try to escape it – and we, therefore, make it so much less overwhelming. It's a little like childbirth: if we are scared of the pain, that anxiety creates tense muscles and higher cortisol levels. And *this* is what makes it hurt more. If we embrace the fact that sometimes, we will experience pain, we somehow soften around the experience, and allow it to pass without turning into suffering.

How can we actively practice embracing what is, rather than avoiding it? For one, we can get better at emotional regulation. Try the following exercise.

The next time you feel an emotion, make your priority to simply become aware of what it is, name it, and *allow it to be*. Don't judge, suppress or diagnose the emotion. Don't try to interpret it or hurry and find a solution or explanation. Don't try to imagine if you are justified in feeling it or not. Don't rank or appraise it, deciding whether it's a good or bad emotion, whether it's too much or too little. Don't get impatient and wonder what's on the other side of the emotion, and start wondering how you can move it along. Just become aware of it. That's all.

You might even like to deliberately say to this emotion, "Hello, emotion, I see you. I'm not afraid of you, don't be afraid of me. Let's sit together."

It sounds a little corny, but notice what it's like to just be with the emotion, as it is. You don't need to summon Buddha-like levels of compassion or totally approve of the emotion, either. You don't have to like it, understand why it's there, or feel as though you're in control of it. You just have to see it.

Easier said than done, however. You might find that the moment you and your emotion are alone together, your brain instantly asks, "Is this it? Come on, give me something more interesting to do!" You may be so automatically drawn to distraction or escape that you don't even notice it at first. But if you are tempted to flee the moment, just bring yourself back. Remember, you're not solving any problems or wrestling any demons. You're just "sitting with."

This exercise sounds *a lot* simpler than it feels to practice in the moment. But that's all you need to do – practice. Just keep being aware. If you find it tricky, there are a few ways to stay anchored in the present without getting distracted by a wandering mind. One way is to "ground" yourself in your sensory perception.

Because your senses are in your body, and your body can only ever be in the present, connecting with your senses will keep you grounded. The next time you're feeling bad, overwhelmed, confused or just generally unhappy, stop and take a moment to reconnect to the present:

Step 1: Focus on your breathing for a moment as you sit somewhere quiet, where you won't be disturbed for a few moments. You could even excuse yourself and step into the bathroom for a moment to gather yourself – you only need a few minutes.

Step 2: Close your eyes and sink into your sense perceptions: sight, sound, taste, touch and smell. Watch as your mind floats around everywhere, and gently ask it to come settle on the things in your immediate environment. For example, you could notice the cold feeling of the tiles on your skin, the tiny specks of water on the faucet, the faint smell of lemon bleach, and the low whirr of the bathroom fan.

Step 3: When your mind wanders, just come back to a sense – any sense. Imagine yourself literally tethering your attention back down to something concrete. The texture of the towel. The feeling of the hard edge of the bath you're sitting on. Don't decide whether anything is good or bad, just notice it.

Step 4: When you're ready, end your sensory contemplation and come back into life again. But before you do, notice if your ruminating mind is a little quieter, and a little less inclined to race from one thought to another.

Exercise 4: Watch your information consumption

Often suffering is a question of overwhelm. As we explored in the exercise above, it almost always accompanies a busy mind that wants to tell stories *about* the present moment, rather than just sit in stillness *in* the present moment. But any time we are hypnotized by the stories our own mind tells us, we are no longer present, and no longer available to life.

The mind is a wonderful servant, they say, and a terrible master. When left to run amok and do whatever it likes, the mind can very definitely concoct a whole world of suffering for you. We not only try to evade pain in the present moment as individuals – we are guilty of this bad habit on a society-wide level. How much of our culture ultimately came about due to someone's distraction, coping mechanism, or denial? And when we engage in the outward manifestations of other people's "thought traffic" do we always do so with perfect awareness of the effect it has on us?

In today's world, many of us find ourselves completely saturated in digital media. TV shows, movies, podcasts, music, social media in all its many forms, the traditional news media, books... everywhere we are surrounded by people saying, essentially, "Look over here. Pay attention to this." And we turn our attention to do just that, we instantly forfeit our ability to decide what we want to focus on.

Let's be honest: the motivations of most of the people who would capture our attention are not noble. Advertisers want to force their way into our awareness, artificially create a need for something, and compel us to buy – even if we never had any intention of doing so. Social media makes us feel bad about who we are. The news makes us afraid, angry, or a mix of both – it's designed precisely for that reason. The content we encounter everywhere is trying to present a particular view of the world to us, and when we absorb it all, we cannot help but take that perspective on as our own.

When we participate in our society's cultural products, we open ourselves up to potential suffering. The ancient Buddhist monks paid close attention to the food they ate, what they wore, and how they filled their waking moments. In their study of mindfulness, they knew that theirs was a discipline rooted in awareness and attention. Their practice was to maintain concentration despite the noise and distraction of the world.

One way to cut down on suffering is to become mindful of the media you consume:

- Before you reflexively pick up your phone or open a new web browser, pause. Notice what you're doing, and why. Are you trying to avoid the moment? What preceded the impulse to distract yourself?
- When you are finished watching a show, reading or listening to something, pause to ask how it has affected you. How do you feel now compared to before you consumed this particular piece of media?
- Can you notice any ways that the media you consume has fed into your "second darts"?

- What do you encounter when you choose not to watch, read, or scroll as normal, and instead just sit with yourself for a moment?

Summary:

- Once we can properly identify suffering for what it is and become aware of it in ourselves, we can begin to manage it better.
- Suffering takes all different forms for each of us, but according to the four noble truths, there is a way to ease and reduce our suffering, by letting go of attachment.
- One way to do this is to practice distinguishing between pain and suffering, first and second darts, and facts or opinions. When you feel upset, slow down and tease apart the situation until you see it as clearly and objectively as possible.
- Try to avoid extremes and black-and-white, all-or-nothing thinking. Watch out for clues to cognitive distortions and bias like absolute terms, catastrophizing and generalization, and instead look for a

balanced path down the middle of extremes. We can achieve this merely by changing our language and how we frame things.

- Counterintuitively, we reduce feelings of suffering by being willing to "sit with" and acknowledge all our feelings, without trying to escape them. We can learn to stay in the present and be aware of how we feel right now, instead of letting our minds get carried away with thoughts of the past or future. One way to keep in the present is to ground in the senses.
- Finally, take care with what you consume, information-wise, since suffering is often a question of overwhelm, or being looped into people's stories and interpretations. Pay close attention to the media you take in, its effect on you, and how these distractions may be helping you avoid your feelings in the present.

4. Stoicism's approach to beat suffering

"A Stoic is someone who morphs fear into prudence, pain into transformation, mistakes into initiation, and desire into undertaking."
Unknown

Tip 1: Control what you can control

The adjective "stoic" has been used to describe asceticism or having a "stiff upper lip" when it comes to suffering. Still, the ancient Roman philosophy of Stoicism has so much more to offer when it comes to understanding and dealing with pain. It's arguable that, through other influential writers and psychotherapists like Paul Dubois in the early 20th century, stoicism has inspired modern-day cognitive behavioral therapy (CBT).

The ancient writings of Seneca, Marcus Aurelias and others favored a practical and dignified approach to the problem of pain. And their findings were not dissimilar to what the Buddhists on the other side of the world were also discovering. They too understood that pain was part of life. However, by focusing passively on it and dwelling on negativity, the pain was essentially amplified, while we forfeited our power to consciously focus on what we valued.

Where the Buddhists focused on tranquility, compassion and a peaceful detachment from the transience of life, the Stoics found refuge in objectivity. What does pain look like when we approach it without layers of fear, resistance, or apathy? Seneca echoes the "second darts" idea when he states, "Do not let us build a second story to our sorrow by being sorry for our sorrow."
Epictetus similarly advises us to, "make the best of what is in our power, and take the rest as it naturally happens." This is seen as

a rational approach to the fact of pain. Again, you might recognize this spirit in the deeply Stoic Serenity Prayer, which has only recently been co-opted by Alcoholics Anonymous and other groups:

"God grant me the serenity to accept the things I cannot change; the courage to change the things I can; and the wisdom to know the difference."

As we did in the previous section, we can consciously work to discern the difference between pain and suffering, between fact and opinion, between sensation and our internal narrative about that sensation. We do not need life to be painless. We need only serenity, courage and wisdom. Some things in life happen outside of our control and without our permission. Some of these things are devastating. Nevertheless, we are always free to focus on what we can control – what else is there to do, really?

Epictetus claims in the Enchiridion (translation by Elizabeth Carter):

"Some things are in our control and others not. Things in our control are opinion, pursuit, desire, aversion, and, in a word, whatever are our own actions. Things not in our control are body, property, reputation, command, and, in one word, whatever are not our own actions. The things in our control are by nature free, unrestrained, unhindered; but those not in our control are weak, slavish, restrained, belonging to others. Remember, then, that if you suppose that things which are slavish by nature are also free, and that what belongs to others is your own, then you will be hindered. You will lament, you will be disturbed, and you will find fault both with gods and men. But if you suppose that only to be your own which is your own, and what belongs to others such as it really is, then no one will ever compel you or restrain you. Further, you will find fault with no one or accuse no one. You will do nothing against your will. No one will hurt you, you will have no enemies, and you will not be harmed."

Though the language here may be strange to modern ears, when Epictetus talks about "lamenting" and being "disturbed" we could arguably substitute the word "suffer" or indeed "experience mental illness" depending on our particular theoretical and cultural perspective. Whether you agree with Epictetus' categorization of what is in control and what isn't, the point remains: we suffer when we *confuse* what is in our zone of control and what isn't.

While the Buddhists feel that suffering comes about from misplaced attachment, the Stoics recognize that too little attachment, or inappropriate attachment, is also a source of trouble. For them, we suffer if we:

1. Fail to take control of things that are in our control, or,
2. Think we can take control over what we actually can't.

For example, we may find that our partner behaves in ways we disagree with, or holds opinions we find unfathomable. Maybe they have a bad habit of getting frustrated with or treating us in ways we dislike, despite trying to convince them otherwise. We may start to feel anxious, helpless, angry and obsessed... but why? Not because of the way they are, but because of how *we* are: we wrongly believe that their behavior is our business, or that it's under our sovereign control. It isn't!

In fact, any time you find yourself unhappy and blaming something external (the government, your family, your job, the universe itself...) then you can be sure this is suffering directly caused by an error in your reasoning. Getting unhappy about what is not in your control doesn't not make it more under your control, and only results in you, well, being unhappy. So why do it? For the Stoics, this sort of passive victim mentality worsens suffering, and doesn't do anything to reduce pain.

Similarly, we suffer if something *is* in our control, but we forfeit this sovereignty by failing to act. Perhaps we are the ones with the bad habit, the weird opinion or the inexcusable behavior. It is nobody's responsibility but our own to fix this – and we suffer when we abdicate this responsibility.

If we want a double dose of suffering, we might even do a blend of both: fail to take responsibility for our actions while simultaneously placing that control outside of ourselves. For example, we have a bad diet and are overweight. We not only fail to control our eating habits (error 1), we also blame external factors for causing our problem, thus ensuring we never take responsibility for it (error 2).

One excellent way to start reducing these kinds of errors in your own life is to ask: is this *mine*?

Is something under your domain of control or not? Is it your responsibility or not? Motivational speaker Byron Katie has her own version of this enquiry. The next time you feel yourself suffering, go quite inside and ask yourself:

Is this my business? (is it in my zone of control?)
Is this their business? (Is this in someone or something else's control?)
Is this God's business? (basically, is this completely outside of anyone's control?)

We can only pragmatically do something about the first. The rest? Like the serenity prayer says, we need to accept.

Tip 2: Be Grateful

It is a mistake to think that Stoic philosophy is gloomy or pessimistic. Rather, the idea is that you actively remove your investment of attention from all those things you cannot hope to change. The energy you free from ruminating over what will not change, can be used to either create what you want – or appreciate how your life is already great just the way it is.

Calmly submitting yourself to your fate doesn't sound very inspiring, and many people dislike the Stoic ideology since it seems to suggest that we should be resigned and passive. Nothing could be further from the truth! Instead, acceptance *frees* us – from struggling against pain instead of rationally approaching it as a fact of life.

One way of reducing suffering is to focus not just on what is in your control, but what is actively going well for you at the moment. Have you ever noticed how amazing it feels to eat after getting really hungry, or how deliciously warm your house suddenly feels after you've been outside in the cold for a long time? The warmth of your house or the tastiness of the meal might not have been something you relished as much had you not actively experienced its absence beforehand.

This is the principle behind what is called negative visualization. There are many versions and approaches to using negative visualization, but this ancient technique is the counterintuitive practice of imagining that *things could be a lot worse.* The effect is that you cultivate more acceptance and contentment for the life you do have, in much the same way as you appreciate food more after being hungry.

Though it is popular today to dwell on positive imagery and engage in affirmations, the Stoics went the other direction. By imagining the worst, we do a few things:

1. We desensitize ourselves to pain, so we are not surprised or unprepared

for it. This constitutes a kind of training towards mental toughness.

2. We compare our current moment against that, and realize how good we have it right now. This inspires feelings of gratitude and wellbeing.

Let's look at an example. In the morning, you could wake up and immediately zone your attention in on the fact that the weather isn't what you want it to be, that it's Monday and that you're tired and cranky. None of these things, of course, can really be changed – except to some extent your bad mood. You might decide to dwell on how bad you feel, or look into the bathroom mirror and force yourself to say an affirmation. Maybe you say something like, "Every day and in every way, I am getting better and better." The trouble is, when you compare this affirmation to what you actually feel, it may seem completely phony. You don't quite believe it, and in fact, it makes you feel even worse about everything.

If you use negative visualization, however, you don't do this. You turn your attention to the fact that you completely overlooked all the amazing things in your life that morning to focus on everything that wasn't working. You ignored your amazing spouse sleeping next to you in bed (and your comfy bed), and you ignored the fact that you are going to a highly coveted job that pays you well and stimulates you mentally.

To practice negative visualization, you could spend a moment to vividly imagine that you have no spouse at all, and are alone. Or, imagine that they are ill with cancer and will die within a month. You could imagine that you don't have your job, and are struggling with money. You could remember having to do this in the past, and remind yourself of just how bad it was to be financially insecure. You could glance over at your bed and see your plush, warm bed, and in fact realize how comfortable your entire home is. You could dwell on the fact that in parts of the world, some people can only dream of such comfort and luxury…

If you practice this technique often enough, the idea is that you start to gain a different perspective, and appreciate what you have. You really internalize the idea that you are owed nothing in life, and that when you grumble and focus on daily irritations and disappointments, you dishonor all the ways you are blessed.

Another variation on this practice can help you find gratitude and perspective and make transient worries easier to bear, which is to deliberately seek out discomfort. This is perhaps the approach most alien to modern readers, but it achieves an additional benefit:

3. If we routinely embrace, endure and accept pain, we realize that's it's not so bad, and that we are more than able to tolerate it and survive.

Sounds dramatic, but imagine an example. You get up and immediately jump into an ice-cold shower. No, you're not being masochistic. The shower is cold and unpleasant. One might argue it's *painful*. But in deliberately seeking it out, we give ourselves the chance to work with and practice a considered attitude towards suffering. Can we endure pain without letting it overwhelm and control us? Is it really the end of the world to temporarily not be perfectly comfortable?

Your cold shower has other benefits. It's a practice for developing discipline and teaching yourself that momentary discomfort is not something to constantly fear and flee. In fact, you might start to crave that blissful moment when you step out of the shower and into the relatively warm room. The "pain" is invigorating. Your senses are sharpened. Where you might have had a nice warm shower and wasted the pleasure by ruminating on something that happened yesterday, the cold shower brings you smack bang into the moment. Not many people would call a cold shower a meditative practice, but it sure is one way to force your attention to the present!

The next time you are hungry, choose to delay satisfaction for a moment. Embrace hunger. Is it so bad to not always get what you want? And isn't it great to realize that you can maintain dignity, self-control and calm even if your every whim is not constantly satisfied? Fasting was traditionally and religiously not about food –

it was about sharpening the mind, spiritual cleansing and recalibrating one's attitude towards desire, craving, and fulfilment. The next time you want to complain, simply imagine that you were completely robbed of the thing you're whining about. You're like the farmer with 83 problems. Have you been taking something for granted?

If you practice this often enough, you may start to discover something very exciting: that pain, discomfort and dissatisfaction can be powerful tools you can use to cultivate wisdom, discipline and contentment.

Tip 3: Take action

Stoicism is not a perfect philosophy. It emerged from a cultural and historical period very different from our own – a world of slavery, empire, war, famine, plagues and social injustice. How do we reconcile acceptance for what we cannot change with the moral duty to make a difference in the world and fight for what is right? Are there some things in life we should *not* accept, but rather rail against?

Each of us has to find a comfortable compromise between activism and ambition on the one hand, and helpless, resigned passivity on the other. The big question here is how we really determine if something is out of our control or not. Is it really a black-and-white thing? How can we tell?

For example, there were periods in history and in many regions of the world where slavery was considered a fact of life. In fact, slavery exists today. The Stoics would have advised a literal slave to observe the fact of their enslavement and accept it, since it could not be changed. This would be considered rational. Then again, we know now that the concept of slavery has only been challenged because of people unwilling to accept that it is in reality a part of life. There are, in other words, different opinions about what constitutes "out of our control."

The Roman philosophy cared deeply about civil participation (for wealthy male landowners, at any rate) and thought it a moral responsibility to act according to one's conscience. And today, all our best loved thought leaders, innovators and spiritual teachers push enthusiastically against the assumption that humankind can't be held to a higher standard.

How do we accept what genuinely cannot be changed, without growing resigned? How do we empower ourselves to change while not inviting more suffering into our lives?

There is one pragmatic way to forge your path ahead: take action. Seek evidence for the decisions you wish to make in your life, form hypotheses, and test them. Observe the effect of your actions, and adjust accordingly. Be patient and dedicated, never allowing yourself to get side-tracked by complaining, helplessness or despair.

Action is grounding, and it always empowers, if it comes from a considered and responsible place inside you. Observe the world around you, take action according to your principles, and then let it be. If you look at a completely corrupt institution, you may realize that 95% of it is rotten and cannot be redeemed. You do not despair about this fact, but simply focus on the 5% - what can you do? When you are alone with yourself in bed at night, you are not overwhelmed by difficulties because you know in your heart you've done what you can.

The Stoic philosophy can seem cold and individualistic to the extreme. It is a philosophy heartily embraced by entrepreneurs and champions of a kind of "dog-eat-dog" conception of the world. But one could argue that the goal of Stoicism was never to simply stand *outside* life, safe from any negative emotion. We can also use our energy to choose – and we can choose to improve the world, to help our fellow human beings, and to create a vision of reality that we value.

The ancient focus on survival, mental toughness and endurance can be updated for our current reality. Marcus Aurelius tells us to, "Meditate often on the interconnectedness and mutual interdependence of all things in the universe." Have sympathy and kindness for others, and realize that you are empowered to take action to *create good*.

Sometimes, we encounter pain and can do nothing but say, "hello, pain. I see you."
But sometimes, we encounter it and can say, "this doesn't have to be this way. I can *change* you."

Again, we need the wisdom to know the difference. When we are in a seemingly dire or hopeless situation, we can almost always lessen our suffering by taking positive action according to our values. When you choose good even in the face of evil, you ennoble yourself, and "be the change you wish to see in the world" as Gandhi asked us. Just because we are focused on bravely accepting what we don't like, and surviving a world we are not in control of, it doesn't mean we can't deliberately look for beauty, and train our focus onto it.

In *Mediations*, Marcus Aurelius says:

"We should remember that even Nature's inadvertence has its own charm, its own attractiveness. The way loaves of bread split open on top in the oven; the ridges are just by-products of the baking, and yet pleasing, somehow: they rouse our appetite without

our knowing why. Or how ripe figs begin to burst. And olives on the point of falling: the shadow of decay gives them a peculiar beauty."

Can we find beauty, meaning and joy even in those things we don't necessarily like, understand or feel in control of?

One way to lessen suffering and remind yourself of your own agency is to take action – even small action. Make your action a dignifying one that highlights the beauty and goodness in the world. Even if nothing at all in your situation changes, *you* may be transformed within.

You could ask, "what is under my control here, and what isn't?" but another way to ask the question is, "**what can I do here to elevate this situation?**" Because there is always something! We always have under our control the ability to speak kindly, to be generous, to forgive, to seek to understand, to create joy and laughter, to find the gentler interpretation rather than the harsher one.

Therefore, compassion can be seen as a rational approach to life. Even if you find yourself answering the question "what can I control?" with "absolutely nothing" it doesn't mean you cannot still smile, be helpful, and try to add value anyway. In this way, we cultivate acceptance and not passive resignation – our acceptance is an active, conscious choice, not something we do because we can't do anything else.

German Muslim footballer Mesut Ozil was once playing a game when fans of the opposition threw a piece of bread at him. Instead of kicking it aside, he picked it up, kissed it, touched it to his forehead, and gently set it aside before continuing to play. What was a disrespectful gesture was thus quietly transformed; he explained that food was not to be wasted in his religion, and his gestures were a way to remind himself to show gratitude to God.

Did this do anything to undo the taunt by the rude fans? Did his action make any material difference to the world? No. The fact of their behavior remained what it was. And yet, his action, though small, was powerful.

Tip 4: Weigh up the costs of struggling

Pushing against things we can't control seems irresistible at times. We rant and rail and complain. We feel it is unfair, unbearable, unjust. But what we can forget is that this attitude comes with a cost. While we are so focused on what is not going our way, we are oblivious to how our struggle itself is a big part of the problem. As the Stoics would say (and the Buddhists, for that matter!), it's not the pain that is our problem, but our resistance to the pain.

Would we be so willing to complain and find fault and struggle if we knew that it was actually making things worse for us?

The problem is that the human brain is wired for a certain kind of negativity. When it zooms in on the worst aspects of a situation, seeking out the problems and highlighting everything that is not right, it thinks it's helping. In many ways, it is! But although struggling and mental resistance are automatic, easy and even biologically inbuilt, it doesn't mean that it's rational or that it makes our lives better.

One way to get out of this bind is to keep consciously reminding yourself to weigh up the benefits and costs of both struggling and acceptance. Once you do this consciously, you can make a deliberate, rational choice for yourself. Usually, we ignore the costs of struggling, but once you grasp the futility of pushing against something which won't move, you won't want to waste that energy again!

Let's look at an example. Imagine one night, on a dark and unlit street, you accidentally run over a dog that dashes across the road. You instantly feel racked with guilt and sadness, and are shaken up for days. You could dwell on this incident and beat yourself up about it, almost punishing yourself with the guilt trip, telling everyone you meet about the incident and how horrible it was. Or, you could take a step back and have a good look at your predicament.

Now, the Stoics would *not* suggest here that all you need to do is pretend everything's fine since the fact of the dog's death cannot be changed. You are sad, and that is also a fact of the situation. You could calmly ask yourself what you could do to better your situation – i.e. what actions you could take. In the short term, of course, you could report the accident and do what you could to notify the owners, as well as move the dog out of the road so that it doesn't endanger anybody else's safety. You could maybe commit to drive a little slower on that road or be extra careful in general, but the fact remains that it was a random accident that you could do little to avoid.

From this point on, you have a choice: you can continue to focus on the sadness and guilt, or you can accept what happened and move on. Yes, it is a choice! You can still feel sad, and you can still wish the dog hadn't been run over. But if you notice yourself in that thought spiral, you can stop and ask yourself, "do my thoughts do a single thing to bring the dog back to life?" In fact, look at what your thoughts are achieving – likely making you miserable. And really, the world does not benefit from your misery!

Now it's true that nobody ever succeeded in turning off their emotions like a tap just because they made the right argument against it. But we do have control over how much we entertain those emotions, how much we focus and dwell on them, how much we fan the flames and keep them burning.

There is nothing that will cause more suffering in life than vehemently insisting that life be other than what it is. If you can improve your situation, use your emotional energy to do that. If you can't, that energy should go towards maintaining your own serenity and self-control. Think of it this way: the thing you're resisting is still going to be what it is, no matter what you do. If you are full of angst and resistance, the situation is what it is, and if you are calm and accepting, the situation is what it is. So, you might as well be calm and spare yourself the energy.

For those of us who feel like acceptance is a little too close to apathy or condoning what we don't like, a subtle mindset shift might help. The Stoics encourage us to gently turn our attention to those areas of life where we do have some control to act and improve things. So, you could ask what life has already given you that can help you cope with your pain. We all have strengths and virtues, we have support networks and the wisdom of other people, we have tools and coping mechanisms, and we can always learn and equip ourselves with knowledge. What are they?

You may not be able to do anything to help the situation right in front of you, but that doesn't mean you can't find any purpose or sense of meaning elsewhere. Intentional and conscious positive action is powerful stuff, even if it's only dimly connected to the problem causing you pain. If you really found yourself eaten up by the accident, you could get in touch with the authorities to see about having a bright streetlight installed to illuminate that dark corner. You could find the dog owners and show them kindness, or perhaps simply offer to help them adopt a new dog. You could donate to an animal charity or volunteer at the local dog shelter. If you were feeling upset and turning the same thoughts around and around in your head, you could simply force yourself to stop and go for a run instead. At the very least, you'll be distracted and give yourself something productive to focus on.

Summary:

- The Stoics, like the Buddhists, understood that pain is just a part of life, and taught that we need to retain quiet, dignified serenity in the face of adversity, focusing on what we can control, while accepting what we can't. One way to practice the Stoic philosophy is to carefully consider your zone of control or, as Byron Katie suggests, identify what is your business, the other person's business, and God's business.
- Another technique is to use negative visualization to develop gratitude for everything you already have. By imagining that things could be a lot worse, you re-calibrate your expectations and focus more with

appreciation on the present. We also desensitize ourselves to discomfort and learn that we can, in fact, endure it.

- One way to empower ourselves in the face of life's pain is to take action. Action grounds us. We can always seek to elevate the situation we find ourselves in, draw on our strengths, and work with what we have. We can choose to build, create and solve problems. We can do this if we stop wasting energy on those things we have no hope of changing.

- Finally, we can become cognizant of the fact that resistance and struggle come with a cost, and inevitably cause us to suffer, all while doing nothing to improve our lives. Though our brains may be primed for a certain kind of negativity, we can always choose to create meaning, do a good deed or take productive action to improve things.

5. Frankl's approach to suffering

Viktor Frankl is an Austrian psychotherapist and famed author of the inspirational book Man's *Search for Meaning*, which details his experiences in a Nazi concentration camp. In this book, Frankl shares his insights from his time spent in four different camps, and explains the basis for a theory he would call Logotherapy, a therapy centered around the creation of meaning.

If we are talking about suffering, then Frankl experienced it. Terror, sickness, starvation, despair, and the threat of death plagued his daily life for three years. In those walls, Frankl encountered something more terrifying than mere physical pain – he had to face the senseless brutality of his fellow man, the feeling of deep anguish and the loss of hope for anything better.

He speaks about looking all around him at others who collapsed into this doom and misery. They stopped believing in a future, and their faith in themselves and humanity in general withered. But here, Frankl noticed other things, too. He noticed that not everyone succumbed and that some people, seemingly despite all odds, repeatedly chose kindness, hope and forgiveness. These are the people that survived. He says that the lesson he was taught was that "it did not really matter what we expected from life, but rather what life expected from us. We needed to stop asking about the meaning of life, and instead think of ourselves as those who were being questioned by life – daily and hourly."

The challenge of existence, then, was to create an active life – meaning one where he finds and serves his purpose, creates, and does ennobling and positive work. This fulfils us and gives us the strength to face adversity. Frankl also claims that it is our responsibility to craft our own moral attitude and behavior. To develop our own philosophy and to live by our own ethics. And, this had to accommodate suffering, not avoid it. In fact, for Frankl, suffering was a big part of the picture: "If there is meaning in life at all, then there must be a meaning in suffering. Suffering is an ineradicable part of life, even as fate and death. Without suffering and death human life cannot be complete."

Man's struggle with suffering, then, is not a mistake but an opportunity to seek and create something deeper and more meaningful. We all have the choice to behave with dignity, no matter how intense our suffering. We all have the option to choose our values – even to seek to be grateful to our suffering for highlighting those values for us. Frankl might have argued, after all, that his touching and eloquent embrace of the role of suffering came about because of his experiences and not in spite of them.

> *"The experiences of camp life show that man does have a choice of action. There were enough examples, often of a heroic nature, which proved that apathy could be overcome, irritability*

suppressed. Man can preserve a vestige of spiritual freedom, of independence of mind, even in such terrible conditions of psychic and physical stress [...] We who lived in concentration camps can remember the men who walked through the huts comforting others, giving away their last piece of bread. They may have been few in number, but they offer sufficient proof that everything can be taken from a man but one thing; the last of the human freedoms – **to choose one's attitude in any given set of circumstances, to choose one's own way ... It is this spiritual freedom – which cannot be taken away – that makes life meaningful and purposeful***.*"

Or, as Nietzsche claimed, "to live is to suffer, and to survive is to find some meaning in suffering."

In Frankl's days of suffering, he found that there was always a choice: even when all action was prevented, you could still determine the contents of your own mind.

He describes being forced to use positive visualization to inoculate himself against the daily tedium and pain. Like the Stoics, he, too, believed that pain lessens dramatically when we are objective and step back. Observe them from afar.

Frankl survived the camps and lived to tell his story, and his repeated conclusion is that love is humankind's ultimate goal, and the deepest purpose and meaning to our lives. Even if we have nothing left in the world at all, we can still choose to love. We can still choose honor and dignity and gratitude.

For Frankl, when we accept that life entails suffering, it gives our lives meaning. Our opportunity as unique individuals living on this planet is then to find an opportunity in the way we bear this burden. There is no question of giving up the burden – our redemption comes in how we carry it, and for what purpose. The *why* tells us *how*.

He who knows how to suffer has mastered everything. Importantly, this is not abstract but real and practical. Modern people are plagued with a lack of meaning and existential emptiness. In this void of meaning, we may succumb to others' will and do as they do. "One should not search for an abstract meaning of life. Everyone has his own specific vocation or mission in life to carry out a concrete assignment that demands fulfilment. Therein he cannot be replaced, nor can his life be repeated. Thus, everyone's task is as unique as is his specific opportunity to implement it. Rather, each man is questioned by life and he can only answer to life by answering for his own life; to life he can only respond by being responsible."

Suffering remedy 1: Find your purpose

Frankl believed that we find meaning in one of three ways:

1. We can work, act or create something of value
2. We can truly encounter another human being
3. We can adopt a certain attitude to our suffering

It's this last route that we are interested in. When we are confronted with an uncomfortable, painful or unjust situation, we have a choice. We can take the opportunity to strengthen our character, and ask what it is that we stand for. We all have immense potential within us, but we must consciously choose to take what we are given and transform it, elevate it, and learn from it. Suffering better means that we don't wish for life to be easier, but for ourselves to be stronger.

Frankl is not suggesting an easy "think positive" solution or encouraging us to make the best of things – can you imagine how hollow this is in the face of the suffering he encountered? Rather, we are each invited by suffering to be better. To choose our own path out of it. To make something of our experiences, according to our values and intention. How we do this depends on us – for some, it will be an exercise in power and will, for others, a creative endeavor, and for still others, a spiritual challenge to be met with love and acceptance.

So, what is your character? What are you made of?

Any truly wise and accomplished person will speak fondly of the pain they've been dealt, the truths this pain showed them, and the lessons they were forced to learn. It's not that pain provides meaning, but rather our engagement with it. It doesn't matter who you are, what your resources are, or how bad you are suffering. At any point, we can *all* take up this work. We can choose our attitude. And we can do this in a very practical way by anchoring into our values.

Here are some questions that can help you zoom in on your unique power to create your own meaning and purpose:

- To what end would you be happy to endure any suffering? In other words, what in this world is so valuable to you that you can imagine sacrificing anything for?
- When have you felt most fulfilled, joyful and at peace in your life? What were you doing?

- What perspective can you offer the world that is 100% unique to you?
- When you are close to leaving this earth, by what standard will you measure your time here? Exactly how will you know you have had a full and meaningful life?
- What story do you want to tell about the adversity you've experienced in life so far?
- At the end of the day, what kind of a person are you, and what do you stand for, no matter what?

Suffering is something that can teach us to find meaning, but it goes the other way around, too: digging deep into our own values and purpose is something that makes suffering easier to bear. Let's look at some examples.

Most people would say that one of the most painful experiences in life is processing the death of a loved one. We can imagine an even more painful situation if we think about the kind of death people most think "shouldn't" happen – the death of a child. A couple could lose their young child and be devastated. For years they would mourn, feeling like the universe had dealt them the unfairest, cruelest blow possible. They could fill up with resentment, bitterness, and deep despair at the unchangeable fact that their child is gone and will never, ever come back.

But this couple could, in time, digest this pain and make something sweet and beautiful out of it. If you speak to them in ten or twenty years, they may say, "We never stop missing her, and the pain never goes away. But her passing taught us to appreciate the time we did have with her, and to never take the beautiful things in life for granted." The couple might say that their pain was like a crash course in finding meaning. When their whole world fell apart, it was a matter of urgency to go inside and ask themselves. "what really matters, then?"

Perhaps their spiritual faith is deepened. Perhaps they realize they had taken things for granted and want to change their lifestyle to prioritize what matters. Maybe they learnt to humble themselves, to allow their community to support them, and to work on their marriage to pull each other through.

Similarly, a bad breakup could leave you with way more clarity about the kind of person you do want to meet and the person *you* want to be when you discover them. You may have never realized before then just how important certain beliefs and values were until you engaged with the pain of that breakup.

A medical scare or prolonged illness may force you to confront the fact you are not currently living with integrity and purpose, and are allowing your unique potential to go unfulfilled and unexplored. Importantly, all of this insight and meaning-making would not be able to happen without *acceptance*. If we fight against and resist the pain we feel, we are always trapped in a reactive, passive mode, feeling like a victim of life. But this just prolongs the pain and delays the insight to be gotten from that pain. We never give ourselves the chance to say, "*This is the way it is*. Can I accept that? What now?"

Suffering remedy 2: Compassion

No matter what we feel we have lost, we never lose our ability to choose kindness and compassion, for ourselves or others. We may not like the adversity or injustice life throws our way, but we can survive it. We can focus on what is good in our lives, and this steadies our mind and helps us maintain our purpose and sense of meaning regardless of what is happening around us.

We can also recognize that great developments in mankind's trajectory here on earth have always happened when people refuse to catastrophize, give up, despair or collapse into blame and self-pity. In fact, human beings are capable of great beauty, mercy, inventiveness and resilience – if they choose it. In this context, as with the Stoics, action is redemptive and grounding. Action gives purpose and direction. And one of the greatest actions we can take is to show kindness.

If somebody treats you badly, pause and decide whether you want to harbor hate and resentment for them in your heart. You might not be able to do anything about what they have chosen, but you can still choose. You can rise above it and forgive, assume the best and let it go. Similarly, if you mess up somehow, don't get too caught up in self-flagellation and guilt. Take very seriously your responsibility for learning what you can and making amends, but don't get too attached to the idea of yourself as a hopeless cause!

If somebody treats you well, realize that their act of kindness, no matter how small, is always within each of us as an unfulfilled possibility. Grab hold of it, be grateful, and do whatever you can to amplify that in the world around you. Pay it forward, and gift the same compassion you were given to somebody else.

Frankl doesn't sugar-coat human nature. He saw both profound cruelty and profound compassion and sweetness in the people he was imprisoned with. "Life in a concentration camp tore open the human soul and exposed its depths. Is it surprising that in those depths we again found human qualities which in their very nature were a mixture of good and evil?"

Frankl believed there were good people and bad people in every group of human beings, and that people could also contain a mix of both. We don't need to rail against the fact that some people are cruel and vicious, and unfair. Our only business is to focus on who we want to be – and we can decide to run our lives according to higher moral values.

There is an urban legend about an attempted break-in. A family were sitting at the dinner table eating, when a man breaks into the house, drunk and violent. Realizing that the house is not empty, he panics and starts threatening them, demanding they give him everything they have. The wife stands up calmly, fetches a plate of food and a glass of wine and hands it to the man, inviting him to come and sit at the table. Overcome with humility and touched by her kindness, the man collapses into floods of tears. He sits with them at the table and apologizes profusely, explaining how his life has hit rock bottom, that he desperately needs help, and that he's so, so sorry for everything he's done.

A cynic will hear this story and think, "Well, what if he decided to just kill them all? Their compassion doesn't mean much then, does it?" But in fact, that's precisely where their compassion has the most meaning. The family don't show kindness for any other reason than wanting that to be what they create in the world. The story may seem to frame the intruder's apologies and remorse as a kind of prize to win by being compassionate, but the value in kindness is there whether others receive it or not.

When we are kind, we also do so because it elevates *us*. Because it makes true the claim that we can create the world we want. We can choose compassion for no "reason" at all. And we can forgive not because of what others "deserve" but because we value our own peace of mind and open-heartedness more than we value clinging to pain.

One unexpectedly powerful way to become masterful at dealing with life's pain is to just let kindness soften it a little. Treat pain like the family treated the intruder – as something deserving of kindness, with you willing to make a place at the table for it, even if it might hurt you. This kind of compassion is not only abstract, but it's also real. It finds its home in concrete action. The next time you feel pain and suffering, try a few of these ideas to remind yourself of your ability to choose your own attitude and take action to reflect it.

Tip 1: Try not to take things personally. Sometimes, there is simply no sense to be found in some people's actions, or even in natural events and phenomena. We suffer when we try to understand or figure it all out, or else look inside to find out what we did personally to deserve it. The next time a bit of bad luck comes your way, shrug it off and say out loud to yourself, "this is not about me." A driver cut you off in traffic? That's his business. It didn't happen **to** you, it just happened. Then let it go.

Tip 2: Try to forgive people who you feel have wronged you in the past. One easy way to do this is to remind yourself of all the ways *you* have hurt others in your life – often unintentionally. Really grasp that you were just doing the best you could at the time. Now take that insight and apply it to the person who hurt you. Can you see how their behaviors were a reflection of their own trouble? Commit to not carrying that trouble with you any longer.

Tip 3: If you find yourself in a rotten situation that you genuinely cannot change or budge even a little, then start thinking of the people involved, and how you show them a little humanity anyway. Offer your help, give a compliment, or simply smile where it would have been easy to scowl. See if there's just one concrete action you can take to make everyone feel a bit better. Sometimes, we can change the whole course of the world by simply adopting a positive mindset, showing others that it's possible, and inspiring them to find that choice in themselves.

Summary:

- Viktor Frankl experienced extreme hardship and suffering and, from this, developed his own theory about how many searches for and creates his own meaning. Frankl's experiences taught him that suffering pushes human beings to find meaning and purpose in their lives. To survive, in other words, is to find meaning in one's suffering.

- Frankl believed that struggle with suffering is an opportunity to seek and create something deeper and more meaningful, identify values and principles, and even deepen one's spiritual understanding.

- Instead of searching for meaning externally, we have to look at our own unique strengths and calling in life, and hear what life demands from us, rather than making demands of it. This means that we need to take concrete action.

- Frankl thought that there were 3 ways to find meaning in life: We can work or create something of value, we can truly encounter another human being, or we can make meaning out of our suffering.

- One way to do this is to fine-tune your own unique purpose. Suffering can force us to look closely at what really matters to us most in life, but knowing our values also allows us to suffer better.

- Another remedy for suffering, according to Frankl, is to have compassion, and to be guided by love. Frankl sees love as mankind's highest possibility, and when we choose kindness and empathy, we can take any form of suffering and redeem it.

6. Suffer better, suffer less

We've taken a close look at three powerful and effective approaches to life's suffering: the Buddhist's perspective, the philosophy of the Stoics, and Viktor Frankl's logotherapy ideas about turning suffering into meaning. You may have noticed plenty of overlap between these, or, more accurately, you might have seen what is essentially the same idea reworked in different cultures and historical contexts. Each of them points, in its own way, to our freedom, responsibility and conscious choice about how we approach the inevitable pain of life. None of these approaches tells us that pain is something we can or even should eliminate from our experience.

We are told by each of these philosophies that action counts. We choose our attitude, and then we demonstrate that attitude by taking action in the world around us. In this chapter we'll consider more deeply some of the tips and techniques we can use right now, whether we're dealing with minor daily irritations or profound loss and suffering on a bigger scale.

The question is, **how** shall we experience pain? We *will* experience pain, and the previous chapters has outlined the attitude we can take towards that pain. But now what? What do we *do* with all this knowledge? In this chapter, we'll look at five practical tips and techniques to use when (note, not if but when!) you next experience pain, disappointment, loss or discomfort.

Tip 1: Get good at reframing

We looked at this when we considered the big (sometimes enormous!) difference between pain and suffering, i.e. our stories and narratives about what that pain is. Viktor Frankl sees that humans are built for telling these kinds of stories, and he encourages us to use that power for good, and rewrite the story of pain so that it's one of compassion, dignity and love.

Reframing might be one of the best things you can learn to do when it comes to pain. Our body receives and interprets signals from our environment that alert us to danger, but this is a very lean process – all the *additional* messages we tell ourselves are unnecessary, and completely under our control.

Consider, for example, the "rule" about what counts as pain in the first place. *Why* are you responding to something in the environment? If you're a modern human, you almost never encounter true physical threat.

Basically, the technique of reframing is telling yourself that you don't always have to take your own word for it. It is usually our rules and stories that make us decide something counts as pain – if we remove those stories or rewrite them, suddenly there may not even be pain anymore!

Here's an example: a friend forgets your birthday. You immediately feel hurt and angry. But rewind a little, and you'll see there's something before the hurt and angry feelings, and that is the mind-frame that told you, "If someone forgets your birthday, it means they don't care about you." It's *this* that has caused your reaction, not your friend. But if you can step back a little, you can query this. Is it really true? Can you know that for absolute certain?

You can probably think of evidence for the fact that your friend really does care about you. And you can also imagine that there are people you care about to who you've nevertheless forgotten to wish a happy birthday. In other words, don't just assume that your interpretation is obvious or correct. The pain you may feel is real – but challenge your rules for deciding on why you feel that pain! If you do, you might discover that you are suffering needlessly. There isn't any problem.

Consider a different example. Your friend forgets your birthday, but when you talk to them about it and think it all through, you realize that they have become much less invested in your friendship, and, well... they forgot because they genuinely don't care as much about you anymore. This could make anyone feel rejected or upset, right? But you can reframe here, too. Maybe you speak to your friend, and they say that since having kids, and since getting a promotion at work, life has been busy. You two have moved further apart, you don't share the same hobbies anymore, and keeping the friendship going is proving difficult.

Is this a cause for suffering?

Potential frame A: everyone always abandons you eventually because you're just not an interesting person
Potential frame B: it's a shame, but sometimes good friendships fade after a while just because life gets in the way, and it's nobody's fault
Potential frame C: it's not bad when lukewarm friendships drift out of your life, since they make room for people who are a better match for you as you are right now!

Each of these frames will result in a different set of emotional reactions (without any change to the actual, objective circumstances!). Also, each frame will impact how empowered you feel, and your chances of taking beneficial action going forward:

Frame A: There's nothing to do but feel sorry for yourself. This is getting the most possible suffering out of the situation!

Frame B: A moderate amount of suffering, but you're likely not going to feel completely crushed or immobilized by the realization. In fact, you might find it a relief to forgive, forget and move on.

Frame C: Maybe you don't suffer at all. Maybe you even deliberately decide to go seek out new friendships – should you get in touch with that interesting person you met in your book club?

Whatever situation you're in, try to delay rushing into an emotional reaction before you've examined the "rules" and beliefs you have that could be causing you to suffer. Ask yourself:

- What assumptions are you making? Do you actually have any evidence that they're true?
- What are you not focused on at the moment? What are you forgetting to factor in here?
- Are you "mind reading" and just guessing what others think and feel, or what they intend?
- Have you told yourself some rule about how things "should" be?
- Are you telling yourself that something "means" something else when there is no evidence for that?

Tip 2: See emotional responses for what they are

Let's keep remembering that for most of us modern humans in the world today, there is very, very little that is a genuine threat. Our nervous system evolved from ancestors who had to face survival threats more intense than the ones we face today, but the same neural machinery and endocrine machinery are still there. Luckily for you, you also have a higher brain capable of examining your responses and choosing something different for yourself.

The thing about pain is that it is fleeting. As the Buddhists teach us, all of life is transient. It constantly moves. Our nervous systems were designed to register pain – but then to act to restore equilibrium as quickly as possible. It is in nobody's interests for you to continue hearing that same pain signal over and over again. Rather, pain arises and then dissipates again.

When you're experiencing pain and suffering, you can fool yourself into thinking that it will last forever. That this is just the way life is now. But this is a form of clinging – it is our attachment itself that is maintaining the pain in the moment, and stopping it from moving on. What happens when you just look at feelings of pain, threat and anxiety as they emerge? You may notice that those feelings are just ghosts. Just patterns in the brain, little crackles of electrochemical energy that have no basis in the real world.

Just because we are having a sensation, it doesn't mean that we will *always* have that sensation, and that that is all we are, as people. Depending on our perspective and attitude, we can see pain as a punishing life sentence that floods our conscious awareness… or we can see it as a temporary cloud that passes over the sky. One that can't help but float away again eventually. If you've ever observed a person having a panic attack, you'll know how powerful the mind can be in convincing us that an apocalypse is unfolding when it's actually a perfectly unthreatening, unremarkable day. In this case, all of the apocalypse is happening purely within the mind. It doesn't exist anywhere else. And when those brain signals stop, *there's nothing there anymore.*

We've spoken a lot about dealing with the inevitability of pain in life, but there's a good chance that a lot of what you're calling "pain" is just a phantom in your mind, nothing more substantial than a weird dream. To dig even deeper, some Buddhists will say that all suffering is, in fact, an illusion. To free ourselves from suffering is not to solve the problem of suffering once and for all – it's to realize that suffering never existed in the first place.

Whether you want to go that far with it or not, you could probably benefit from asking yourself honestly whether you're creating suffering for yourself out of thin air. Sometimes, we become attached to feeling bad. It might sound strange, but we are almost convinced that if we feel bad (angry, sad, scared), then we had better carry on being that way. Even though we're not enjoying our suffering, we still hold onto it, almost looking for further reasons to justify it. Have you ever felt yourself deciding that you were in a bad mood, and almost deliberately choosing not to crack a smile at something funny because you were busy being in a bad mood?

Though it's a little cheesy, you can think of emotion as e-motion – energy in motion. Every time you feel something, remind yourself that an emotion's job is to move. It's just like a ripple in a pond. The pond exists, but the ripple is just a temporary movement, nothing more.

Here's how we can best let emotions do what they do and move on:

- Acknowledge them. Embrace and welcome them fully, without resistance, judgment, blame, interpretation, shame, clinging or denial. Don't distract yourself or bully yourself into feeling some other way. Can you find a name for what you're feeling?

- Get some distance in the language you use. Instead of saying, "I'm a miserable wretch" say, "I feel sad right now", or even "there's a lot of sadness at the moment."

- Recognize that you only feel bad right now because previously you felt good… and before that, you felt bad. Is it really the end of the world to have your emotions move and change? Keep asking yourself, "In all this change, what is permanent? What is unchanging?" This is a profound and anchoring question to return to.

Tip 3: Embrace effort and difficulty

The "effort paradox" is what some psychologists call our tendency to want to avoid effort (i.e. be lazy) when hard work is a source of pleasure and meaning for us. Call it human nature to want to take the shortcut or the path of least resistance. But an interesting quirk of how we think is that we also tend to value more those things we've worked hard on. In other words, putting effort into something makes it much easier to deal with – even like.

Benjamin Franklin said that if you wanted people to like you, ask them to do you a favor. When people work for something, they automatically value it more. Taking it further, when something arrives at the end of effort and was quite difficult to win, we seem to think it's more valuable than something that came for free. Researcher Michael Norton at Harvard Business School put his study results down to what he called the "IKEA effect" – when we do things ourselves (for example, build our own furniture), we value them more.

Consider the answers you might get if you asked people to outline their dream life for you. Maybe they would say they want to sit on a tropical beach forever, never having to lift a finger. The truth is (and you can ask any retired person to confirm!) you get *bored* without something to work for. Without a little challenge and friction and effort. Your self-esteem and sense of purpose suffer. You lose motivation and energy. So, there's the irony – hard work can be energizing, and rest can be draining.

How does this apply to suffering? Well, think about the fact that most of us seem to have an unconscious idea about how much suffering is normal and expected in a life. How bad can things get before we feel that we're hard done by? We may have a hypothetical end goal on the horizon, where all of our problems are finally solved, there's no friction, nothing to worry about, and everyone is self-actualized and completely free of angst.

But just reading that should show you how silly this expectation really is!

So far, we've considered a stoic (lower case "c") attitude to grinning and bearing whatever adversity comes our way. Like pain is something to tolerate bravely. But can we also learn to actually appreciate effort and friction for the value it brings to life?

Let's look at examples. Imagine you and your partner occasionally have disagreements. They have the uncanny knack of knowing the most annoying things to say to you, and you seem to push their buttons at times, too. You don't agree, and sometimes you even wonder what planet they're living on. You have moments when you doubt your relationship, and when you feel angry at them. But then, you're forced to communicate, compromise and be humble as you own up to all the ways that you're not quite perfect, either.

If you do this and come back to harmony with that person, you may well value this harmony with them way more than if you had blandly gotten on without any friction ever. Occasional arguments are a challenge. They keep you on your toes and stop you from getting complacent and making assumptions. They remind you that you are dealing with an ever-changing, sometimes contradictory, ultimately unknowable force in the universe – another human being! You need to learn intelligent new skills to work with them, you need to cultivate forgiveness and trust and love, and together you build something stronger than it was before you had your argument. It's hard to imagine people valuing one another more if they have never been "tested" this way, never been pushed to the limits of their skill or understanding or ability.

Similarly, if you were an athlete, you would doubtless think less highly of your sport and your own abilities if your coach insisted on keeping you well within your comfort zone, never pushing too hard. Many people leave good jobs for a related reason: because they are not stimulating enough. Just as Frankl suggested a link between suffering and meaning, we can see that meaning is also connected to effort. To hard work.

The next time you feel that you are experiencing pain or, **ask whether you are**

actually suffering, or whether you are just learning. Is the discomfort you feel just what it's like to change and grow? Can you think of a few things this "suffering" is actually teaching you? Can you think of all the things it's training you to value?

Tip 4: Accept the reality check

We wouldn't be honest if we didn't include one very common source of suffering in life: our own stupidity. What's more, we sometimes suffer purely because of our own actions. Perhaps we've failed to heed warnings and carried on with a bad course, only to have it blow up in our faces. Perhaps we're in denial, and the pain is showing us that we can no longer avoid something. Perhaps we need to be frank about our role in choosing circumstances that are just no longer working. Our body sends pain signals when our hand is on a hot stove so that we can pull our hand away. In the same way, emotional and mental suffering can be seen as a message telling us, "Get away from this situation!"

We will continue to feel suffering until we do.

Think about someone who is in a job that is really bad for them. They are underpaid mistreated, and the hours and workload are ruining their health. Leaving this job would be scary, however, so the person puts it out of their awareness for a while. They still suffer in the job, though. But when they feel bad, they meditate and tell themselves, "Well, suffering is a part of life. What are you going to do? I'm choosing to graciously accept my fate."

Ridiculous, right?

There's one thing such a person can expect here, and that's that the "pain signal" will only get louder. More stress, more health problems. Maybe everything *won't* be OK. Maybe they are not being accepting but rather telling themselves comforting lies to hide the fact that they have chosen not to act to improve their situation.

It's a wonderful thing to be optimistic and to embrace what can't be changed. But as the Stoics teach us, that's only half of the "serenity prayer." We are only encouraged to accept the things we genuinely cannot change. To the full extent that we can take responsible action and shape our lives, we do. We reserve acceptance only for things thing s beyond that.

Sometimes pain and suffering is a messenger that's yelling at you, "it's time to change!" We might be tempted to downplay that or run away from it when we assume that this pain is just part of the natural order somehow. Of course, nobody is suggesting that you collapse into pessimism and bitterness, and declare that life sucks. But if that *is* how you feel, acknowledge it. Accept that that is how you really feel. It may be the first step to realizing that something needs to change for you. And this may have to be a big, serious, genuine change, and not some sugary fairy tale.

This can be a tricky area to navigate, for sure. We need to get good at being honest with ourselves. Remember that a reassuring lie may feel better than a harsh truth, but it won't make you grow, won't add to your understanding, and won't allow you to learn anything. In the long run, the lie creates *more* suffering. In this case, we need to realize that sometimes "suffering" is the right way forward. It's like having a deep cut. You need to clean the wound and dress it so that it can heal, and maybe even get stitches. This will hurt a lot, but if you avoid that pain, you allow the problem to get worse over time, and risk that wound not healing properly or getting infected and leaving a scar. Likewise, you can't pretend that you can just slap on a Flintstones Band-Aid and forget about it!

Here are some questions to help you check in with the function your pain may actually be serving right now:

- If you are honest, is this pain here because of something you've been deliberately ignoring till now?
- Carefully try to understand what your role is in bringing this situation about, *and* maintaining it. There's no need for blame – just see what portion of the problem is due to your actions and choices. Can you write them down?
- Sometimes we avoid facing our feelings because doing so would

compel us to act and make changes. What feelings are you too scared to acknowledge right now, because you're not sure what you'd do with them?

Tip 5: Train for the pain

Think about the attitude that extreme athletes and sportspeople have to pain. They're able to push themselves through punishing ordeals, scale mountains, swim and cycle and run unthinkably long distances, and keep going despite extreme discomfort and pain. Why? And more importantly, why do some others not manage to endure pain as readily?

Kevin Alschuler is a psychologist at the University of Washington School of Medicine, and he was interested in this very question. In 2016, he followed participants as they completed 155-mile-long foot races in desserts across the world. He found a link between each runner's coping strategy and their chances of finishing the run.

What were these coping strategies?

Alschuler found that the most adaptive mindset was one that reframed pain not as pain at all, but as a challenge. The people who fared best simply refused to allow the discomfort to bother them, or they ignored it completely. During painful periods of their long-distance and endurance challenges, the best performers simply distracted themselves and carried on. They seem to quickly accept the reality of the pain but tell themselves that there's no getting rid of it. The options are to keep going or to stop – and for the ultra-elite athletes, stopping just wasn't a viable option. So they didn't even consider it.

This actually isn't quite as difficult as it may seem. It's more a question of what you *don't* do – you don't catastrophize or let yourself dwell on just how bad it is. You don't entertain thoughts of giving up. You just stay in the present and focus on the challenge in front of you. When that's accomplished, you move on to the next one. If the pain's intense, you may need to do this literally second by second. But if you can, you may find that you develop extraordinary resilience and endurance.

Realize that you are not your suffering, and that the pain is temporary. Realize also that you greatly increase those feelings if you focus on them. Instead, hold onto the idea that you have committed to act, and that you will keep acting accordingly, no matter what. Keep it simple.

You don't have to be a pro-athlete or runner to use this mindset. Simply choose not to dwell too much on your own pain, or indulge in drama. Even if things are *really* uncomfortable, are they the end of the world? Can you just relax and get through it? An unpleasant feeling is just that unpleasant. It's not the end of you, and it's not a sign that you should stop.

Imagine that you are studying hard for an important exam and need to put in the hours. You can do whatever you like when it comes to planning and strategizing, but at some point, you'll have to get working, and endure several study sessions that may feel like running a marathon. The tiredness is not the main adversary – your attitude to the tiredness is. You could decide that a bit of fatigue and slightly sore eyes is a Bad Thing and freak out about it, or you could have a quick break, stretch, rest your eyes for a second and tell yourself that you are capable of enduring temporary discomfort.

In emergencies, too, people fare best when they make sure that their lazy, scared or fearful minds get out of the way, so they can think calmly and just do what needs to be done. If someone you loved passed away and you were tasked with all the duties of arranging a large funeral, well, the best way to do it is to see the discomfort, acknowledge it, and simply do what needed to be done without too much drama or overthinking. You could tell yourself, "People are relying on me to take charge here, and I will. It's a challenge I am capable of meeting. I don't have to like it, but I will do it, and I will be fine." Everything beyond that is suffering. If you grit your teeth and curse the responsibility and complain about how unfair it is and how you're too upset to do it and on and on, it doesn't change the fact of the task that is ahead of you. Once you start running that marathon, however, and you just put one foot in front of the other, you will realize something great: that you *can*.

Summary:

- The fourth noble truth encourages us to follow the eight-fold path, i.e. we need to understand suffering but also take concrete *action* towards our intended life every day. We can use proven and effective tools to help us suffer better, and suffer less.
- Firstly, we can learn the power of reframing so that we investigate the "rules" we have for deciding what counts as pain or suffering in the first place. Much suffering disappears when we take our own assumptions and interpretations out of the picture.
- Emotions are fleeting and always changing. When we understand this, we don't cling to one emotion or reject another. It's useful to learn to accept, embrace and name emotions for what they are, so they can flow.
- A third tip is to understand that effort and difficulty don't always signal pain, and rather than being something to avoid, it can be enriching. Get into the habit of asking whether you are really suffering or whether you are just

experiencing the inevitable discomfort of change and growth.

- Realize that sometimes, pain and suffering may be a sign that something needs to change. Pain can be a wake-up call if we heed its message honestly. Not all pain has to be stoically endured. Be frank with yourself about the cause of pain in your life, and what its message is.

- Finally, understand that even raw, blind pain such as the pain experienced by endurance pro-athletes is not the end of the world. Those who fare best tend to have an attitude of "no option." They distract themselves when it comes to discomfort and don't allow themselves to indulge in thoughts of giving up.

7. The Mindset of the Present

John is only sixteen years old, but he feels the weight of the world on his shoulders.

His parents, teachers, and guidance counselor are pushing him to plan one of the most important decisions of his life, his career, right now. He doesn't know what job will make him happy. He doesn't know how much money he needs to earn. He's never even managed a budget! He spends hours ruminating and poring over advice columns and college websites, but nothing seems to help. He's positive that he needs to go to college, but for what?

Should he take a risk on a more interesting but lower-paying career, or should he choose a path with better pay and more job security? Would he be happy if he chose the latter option? What if he chose the former option, and the lower pay left him desperate? What if a good school wouldn't even accept him; would that mar his chances for life?

He's worried—very worried—and not much is helping his anxiety. He spends so much time worrying about his future, trying to figure out the rest of his life, that he starts losing his grasp on what's happening around him. He's stopped talking to most of his friends, and he rarely accepts invitations anymore. Instead, he spends his time reading and worrying, worrying and reading. Soon his anxiety would interfere with his sleep and distract him while studying, lowering his grades and genuinely limiting his chances of attaining his own best future.

Because John can't stop fretting about the future, he's losing his friends, his sanity, and his future.

His mother, Julia, has the opposite problem. When she looks at her current life, she sees little of interest. Feeling empty, she retreats into her mind, relishing the hope and excitement of her high school days. Sure, the work was hard, but overcoming academic challenges was a fulfilling struggle that afforded her the opportunity to triumph. She still wishes she'd spent more time on her studies. Back then, her main priority was maintaining her friendships. She'd stay out late, gossiping and laughing for hours with her friends.

She can't remember the last time she went out with friends. It had to have been years ago. As a stay-at-home mom, her family has become the sum total of her life. Often, she thinks about how different her life could've been if she'd finished her college degree instead of dropping out to get married and become a mother. At the time, it had seemed like a good idea.

She was deeply in love and eager to have kids. Her husband and children still make her happy, but it isn't enough. She wishes she hadn't thrown away all those opportunities. She could have been self-reliant and respected. She could have made a real difference in the world. But now she's a middle-aged parent with a decades' wide gap in her resume. What could she do now?

Career-wise, she was finished. She's made her choices; there's nothing she can do. Julia is so preoccupied with her past decisions and the life she used to live that she hardly notices the joy abounding in her current life. Her nostalgia even prevents her from seeing the opportunities she currently has to improve herself and her life. Being stuck in the past is making her miserable in the present.

Both mother and son have great intentions; it's good to plan our futures, and it's equally good to reflect upon our past. That's how we learn and choose what to do with ourselves. But both went wrong by being so focused on their thoughts that they lost track of the circumstances, responsibilities, and opportunities right in front of them. Focusing on that would let them make the most of their lives.

Author Eckhart Tolle has great insight into the problem of fixating on the past or future; he once said, "All negativity is caused by an accumulation of psychological time and denial of the present. Unease, anxiety, tension, stress, worry—all forms of fear—are caused by too much *future* and not enough presence. Guilt, regret, resentment, grievances, sadness, bitterness, and all forms of non-forgiveness are caused by too much *past*, and not enough presence."

Tolle claims that focusing on the future causes fear that manifests as unease, anxiety, tension, stress, and worry. In other words, fears about what could happen stress us out. Thinking about the future to solve problems turns bad when fear becomes stronger than hope. Fear becomes a problem when, for whatever reason, we can't easily find a satisfying conclusion.

In an ideal world, we would admit that we can't predict or control things and wait to see what happens. But instead, we worry. And worrying produces stress, which releases cortisone and adrenaline into our bodies, leading to higher levels of baseline anxiety and the tight, stiff muscles that come with it. The real pickle is that when we feel bad mentally and physically, like we do when we're stressed, it becomes even harder to solve our problems. This amplifies our stress and our worries, leading to a vicious, self-destructive cycle that keeps us firmly fixated on the future and the horrible outcomes we fear.

Conversely, when we fixate on our failures, whether it's insulting a kid in second grade, failing our driver's test, or a real mistake, like committing a felony, we are failing to forgive ourselves. We are focusing on what we did in the past, on the people we used to be, rather than on who and what we are now. People learn from their mistakes. Improving over time is a good thing, and we can't do that unless we mess up first. But too often, we identify with our guilt and shame; we think our worst decisions define our character.

The past, along with everything we've done, is gone. It can't be changed; it can only be accepted. We cannot allow it to linger, dominating our lives and moods with negativity.

Forgiving ourselves, others, and the world is essential, but Tolle mentions another ingredient for avoiding the negative emotions that erupt when we're immersed in the wrong time: presence. Forgiveness allows us to focus on the present more easily, but what other steps can we take to be more present?

Moving Beyond the Past

Contemplating our mishaps has a certain allure. Unlike present actions, the outcomes of which we can't yet know, the past is resolved. We know the outcome of each action; we've lived through it. We know the emotions and consequences that erupted from our decisions, and we can no longer do anything to fix those mistakes.

This powerlessness can feel liberating because it frees us of the responsibility to act.

We've already made our choice, it's said and done, and relief comes with that sense of finality. If nothing else, it's a stark and comforting contrast to the uncertainty of the future. In a way, it's safer to ponder mistakes and wonder what could have happened if we'd acted differently than to make a decision and act in the present, when more failure may lurk around the bend.

But lingering on the past is a massive waste of time and energy because the present is all we have. We don't live in the past or the future, but in the now. We can't take paths we missed in the past, and we can't know what our current choices will bring until our futures become our present. We can only try our best and make the smartest decisions we can. Anything else is impossible, and holding anyone to impossible standards only invites regret, anger, bitterness, resentment, and hatred—of yourself, other people, and the hand of fate alike.

The first step toward breaking this destructive habit is asking yourself why you're stuck in the past. What emotion is making you return to the past? Do you feel guilty about something you did? Do you regret something you didn't do? Are you resentful about old wounds? Are you bitter that opportunities were taken from you? Pinpoint your grievance, accept that it can't be changed, and forgive everyone—including yourself—for being imperfect.

People make mistakes. While mistakes are frustrating, their existence is inevitable. Often, they're even helpful. Think about it: do you remember the right answers you had on the tests you took in school? Odds are, you don't. You were told you knew what you were doing, so you didn't linger on it. But mistakes stand out. We see that red ink, and we're bothered that we did poorly. This distress encourages us to review the material we missed, and the added weight of having been wrong solidifies the message in our minds. Because we made mistakes, we remember the true answers, the better actions, and the more compassionate approaches more readily. So being wrong is good. If we're willing to learn our lessons, it helps us become better, more successful people.

But what about when people choose to hurt us? We learn from that, too. We can learn to identify and avoid hurtful people and situations from poor experiences in the past. A woman is unlikely to walk back into a particular bar after being pawed like a cat toy by men in that locale, for example. That's a lesson learned. Most of the times that we're wronged can supply us with similar lessons, making us stronger and wiser as we collect life experience.

Bad things happen to everyone, but focusing on being a victim gives all your agency to the past. By contrast, seeing yourself as a fighter or a survivor roots you in the present.

Fighters actively confront their pain, learn from it, resolve lingering emotions, and work toward forgiveness and acceptance. Survivors have finished that work and put their experiences behind them. They know they went through hard times, but they emerged on the other side. They understand that they're stronger, wiser, and more experienced than people who haven't seen those aspects of our world. Neither fighters nor survivors stand down and accept their past defining their present. Instead, they leave it behind and focus on the change they're creating right now.

What's happening right now, for you, in the present moment? You're reading, but where are you? Is it comfortable? Are you hungry or thirsty, and do you have the means to fix it? Are you tired or ill and able to rest soon? What else is going on around you right this second? No matter where you are, it's probably nothing terrible. Most of us live calm, peaceful lives that contain innumerable reasons to be happy. As humans, we're prone to lingering on the few bad moments in every day and getting stuck on errors and disappointments we experienced, but the present moment? That's usually pretty good. We all need to notice that, to appreciate that, more often.

Accepting an Uncertain Future

Anticipating and planning for our future needs is often extolled as a virtue in society, and it's definitely important for us to act in ways that will make our lives easier in later years. For example, when we don't save for retirement, we find ourselves scrambling in desperation when we become too old to perform our jobs adequately. Similarly, investing in our future housing stability by buying a house or our future career options by taking skill-development courses is not only wise but often necessary. When we perform these actions, we are creating a more stable, secure, and comfortable life for our future selves. But even this version of living for the future, commendable as it is, can be overdone.

Consider the case of the diligent young man who lives well below his means, siphons almost all his income into savings and investments, and is hit by a bus at 34. He couldn't have known he was wasting his life—he was doing the "right" thing—but he never got to enjoy the fruits of his labor. His hard work was in vain.

Tomorrow can't be taken for granted by any of us, nor can reaching a ripe old age. Saving is important. Acting to ensure our lasting well-being is indispensable. But delaying all or most of our happiness for the sake of a future that may never come sacrifices the present for the future and drains happiness from life. Balance is necessary. Plan and act *for* the future but live and act *in* the moment.

Imagining our future can help us crystallize our goals and enhance our confidence if we do it in moderation, but goals are only useful when they are followed by real, daily action.

159

When dreams of the future distract us from performing those tasks, they're a waste of time at best. At worst, they're creating dread and despair for our current lives because we aren't living the life we want.

When we do this, we've raised our expectations so high that all we feel is disappointment. Worse, this mismatch between our expectations and what we feel we deserve can quickly lead to anxiety. Will we ever get what we want? Will we ever be good enough? How can anyone make that much progress? These anxious trains of thought can further propel people toward daydreaming, as it makes daily life more and more unpleasant. Avoid this by setting reasonable, achievable, stepwise goals for yourself. When you see yourself getting closer to your goals, it's easy to imagine reaching your final destination.

Keeping our brains too fixated on the future damages our happiness, even when we have modest expectations, if we allow our anxiety to take over. It's easy to be afraid that people will boo us off the stage during a speech or that our car will break down on a long drive.

It's even easier to imagine the hundred ways that we can fail ourselves by not having the strength or character needed to do our work.

But in reality, most people are kind and will accept gaffes, mistakes, or even the occasional calamity. In reality, the world isn't out to get us; it's filled with kind people who are willing to help and a million opportunities that most of us can't imagine until we see them before us. And in reality, most of the things that can go wrong won't go wrong. Wasting our time fretting for hours, days, or years over mistakes and misfortunes that will, in most cases, not happen is needless.

Worries are only useful as a reminder. If you're worried you're going to mess up your speech, stop thinking about it and practice more instead. If you're worried about your car breaking down, make sure to carry your cell phone and sign up for a roadside assistance service. If there is something you can do to prevent misfortunes, do that thing, then let the worry go. You've done your best.

Meanwhile, if you're anxious about something that you can't control or mitigate, there's no benefit in worrying at all; you're better off enjoying life or working to improve your world. After all, it's not like worrying about a potential problem makes that problem any less likely; it only makes you devote more of your life to that event than necessary—and at a critical cost.

Worrying activates the body's stress response, increasing blood pressure, cortisol levels, and the amount of adrenaline pumping through our veins. Combined, these contribute to heart disease, weight gain, insomnia, and some truly unpleasant neurological changes; the effects of these outcomes range from death to improving your likelihood of making poor decisions in the future.

How do we avoid this? Relax a little. Be kind to yourself. Remind yourself that what you "should" do is no more important than what you "want" to do. Treat yourself when you can afford the expense, calories, and lost time. Remember that plans can change and mistakes are not the end of the world. Get enough sleep. Set time aside in each day to enjoy the little things. Without this focus on your present needs, your present life, it's easy to run yourself into the ground and burn out before you even come close to the life you want to live. Go slow and steady; that's the only way to win.

Just don't take it too far. Forgetting the future entirely will make you forget to strive for better things. Similarly, avoiding thoughts of tomorrow can be a way to avoid facing the inevitable change of life. You, your life, your capacities, and your possessions will not remain constant from birth to death. Bodies and minds grow old, people move on, and physical objects break and deteriorate. We must learn to minimize these damages and maximize our gains despite these potentially frustrating facts of life. Giving a thoughtful eye to the future, figuring out a good plan of action, and enacting that plan in our present is the way through. Identify what you need to do and act instead of letting fear develop.

How to Live in the Present

How can we stay in the present? How can we develop our ability to remain conscious of our current environment and actions? Better yet, how can we pull ourselves back to the present when we get stuck lingering on our futures and pasts?

Focus on the present moment. Notice the interactions and processes occurring around you. Quietly observe actions as they unfold and notice your place in the times and locations you experience. Consider any thoughts that arise, but don't linger on them. The point of this exercise is to really notice the world outside of you and how you can shape and change it with your body and mind. This is great to do while baking or performing housework and can transform the experience from an unpleasant task you can't wait to finish into a fascinating exploration of the world we occupy.

Pay attention to your senses while going about your day. When you smell something, consider what you can hear or see at the same time. Notice the feeling of fabric on your skin and the breeze through your hair as you move. Feel sunshine, smell the grass and the flowers you pass, and really notice the complex and nuanced flavors of your food. When we focus on our senses, instead of dismissing the information they offer us, a wealth of riches can be discovered in the most mundane events. It also helps us stay connected to our environment, which keeps us in the moment.

Pay attention to your body. Consider and correct your posture. Scan your body to find areas of tension, then tighten and relax those muscles to relieve stress. Pay attention when you feel hungry or thirsty rather than immediately grabbing some food or drink. Notice whether what you really feel is hunger, boredom, or a need for emotional fulfillment; act accordingly. When we genuinely notice what we feel physically, we become more grounded and less prone to distraction.

Learn to meditate and make it a regular practice. The easiest way to start out is through a simple breathing exercise. Breathe in, noticing the physical sensations of your lungs filling with air. Then breathe out while noticing all of the details of that sensation. The important thing here, as in a lot of meditative practices, is to focus on one thing for an extended period of time. Anything can be a focus of simple, singular contemplation like this, but focusing on breathing is one of the easier ways to start.

However you decide to meditate, know that you will be distracted. Thoughts will arise in your mind. When they do, notice them for what they are and return to the object you're focusing on. Over time, it will become easier to let go of thoughts and focus on a chosen object. Once you gain that discipline, it's a lot easier to dismiss anxious or distracting thoughts in your day-to-day life.

Allow yourself unspeakable, childlike joy. Children explore the world in a simple, naïve, and hopeful manner. They play with toys, make up games, and form attachments with gusto. Reviving some of your childlike fervor by allowing yourself to experience that same joy as an adult can amp up your ability to live without fear, and that's a great way to stay in the present moment.

Write down things you're happy about or grateful for every day. If you make this a consistent practice, you'll find more and more reasons to be glad every day. Often, we take for granted the good things in life, leaving us with painful and unfortunate events to focus on. Forming a habit of noticing the good trains us out of that mindset and makes us appreciate all the good stuff that happens every day. Even better, writing down the details gives us an easy reference sheet to remind us of all the good things that have happened and will happen to us again in the future. It's a lot harder to be carried away by negative thoughts when you have proof of all the good in your life!

When you're getting stuff done, monotask, don't multitask. Monotasking has been shown to increase focus, happiness, and the quality of our work while reducing stress. All of these help our days go smoothly and our goals get accomplished; that makes it easier to appreciate our current lives.

Take small steps toward the life you want. Often, it can feel like our endgame is a million miles away and we'll never reach it. That can make us discouraged, encouraging us to give up. But almost every goal affords us something that can be done to get closer to it, even if it's as small as reading an article or setting up a savings account. Small steps, when put together, allow for a lot of progress. If you work toward your goals for twenty or thirty minutes every day, you'll be who you want to be, doing exactly what you want to do, in no time at all.

Release tension, set intention. This tip comes from the book *High Performance Habits* by Brendon Burchard. To do it, stop between projects or events in your life to take two to three minutes to focus on your breathing, releasing all the tension from your body. Our prior steps about meditating and focusing on your body should help. After you do this, think about how you want to move forward right now. When you do this, you'll find that the tasks you perform in a day transform from an endless series of events to complete into isolated tasks that are approached with singular focus. This will increase your performance by keeping your current task in the forefront of your mind.

When you notice your thoughts drifting unconsciously to the past or future—and you will; we all do—take that drifting as a cue that you need to perform one or more of the focusing tasks listed above. You don't have to give in to the cycle; the distracted thoughts themselves can be your cue to dive right back into the present moment.

Remember, our whole lives exist in the now, and our actions in those successive moments are what we should be thinking about most of the time. That way we notice all the calm, peaceful, joyful things we encounter, and we remember to stay calmly and dutifully on the path that will lead us to our goals.

When we think of the past, it should be to learn a lesson, resolve emotions, or relive a pleasant experience. If we spiral into unpleasantness, we need to engage in actions that will pull us back to the peace and joy of the present moment. Similarly, when we think of the future, it should always be with an eye toward inspiring our current actions and planning our path to our goals. If it isn't directly informing or motivating current actions, it's taking up time for no purpose and we must recall ourselves to the current time. In the end, we can only control the present moment. The past is gone, the future is uncertain, but the life we're living right here, right now? That's real. We control that. Let's make it good.

Summary

- Stay present. It's something we hear frequently, but what does it mean? Simply put, we are more often caught in the past or looking forward to the future. When we are caught in the past, we are affected by things and events that we have no control over. When we are looking forward to the future (excessively, of course), we are also affected by that which we have no control over.

- Author Eckhart Tolle has great insight into the problem of fixating on the past or future; he once said, "All negativity is caused by an accumulation of psychological time and denial of the present. Unease, anxiety, tension, stress, worry—all forms of fear—are caused by too much *future* and not enough presence. Guilt, regret, resentment, grievances, sadness, bitterness, and all forms of non-forgiveness are caused by too much *past*, and not enough presence."

- To let go of the past is to forgive, excuse, and allow for errors. We can learn from the past, and we don't have to experience things in vain. To stop fixating on the future is to accept uncertainty and a certain amount of randomness. We cannot control very much in our lives, and all we can control is our actions and reactions.

- Staying in the present is of course easier said than done, but the practice of meditation is a useful blueprint. It is important to clear your mind and simply lose yourself in a thought, feeling, or sensation. Preoccupation is the worst of sins here, and it can only be defeated with time and practice—and the knowledge that the past does not matter anymore and the future is out of our control.

8. The Balm of Humor by Jason Merchey

A Sense of Humor is an Excellent Coping Mechanism

> *I'm not offended by all the dumb blonde jokes—because I know I'm not dumb. And I'm not blonde.*—Dolly Parton

Yes, the world is one big downer. It seriously brings me low sometimes. I slap my forehead, yell at the television, mumble under my breath, sigh deeply, and sometimes just need a beer. I mean not all the time, but it's hard to watch the news or be on social media with Trump, Putin, COVID, cancel culture, obsessed corporations, and the anger—I feel like America has gotten angrier in the last decade!

I was also born (*cursed? graced?)* with a vibrant and unique sense of humor. When I am at my best, I feel positive and like to kid around, make fun of stuff, and be lighthearted. So yes, I think that *humor* and even *lightheartedness* are indeed values of the wise—not just childish buffoonery. There is a lot to laugh at in this world, and hey, laughing is good for you. In other words, it's an excellent coping mechanism for dealing with "life's slings and arrows."

> *I'm not afraid of death; I just don't want to be there when it happens.* —Woody Allen

A case can certainly be made that humans are survivors; that we are moral creatures; that we are about work, money, status, competition, sex, and adventure. That is certainly true to some degree. And we often take things way too seriously (enter Stoicism and myriad modern self-help philosophies). But, taking a relaxed, joyous, *Don't sweat the small stuff* approach to life is one that humans also seem to possess. Football, video games, walks in the park, and yes, comedy, provide much relief and distraction to Americans. It's an amazing feat of evolution, really, that joking and laughing and acting foolish are hard-wired into us. Take a look at TikTok if you don't believe me!

Indeed, think about how easily human beings *in all cultures* gravitate toward lightheartedness and joviality. Try this on for size: two of the hardest-working, most *serious* cultures (and the bad guys in World War II)—the Germans and the Japanese—are known to really let loose when alcohol is the social lubricant of the evening. Ever seen pictures of Japanese businessmen acting the fool in a sushi or karaoke bar? How about Germany's *Oktoberfest*—it is virtually synonymous with letting loose and enjoying oneself. Think of the popularity of comedy movies and television shows. Who would listen to a *minute* of Woody Allen or Tyler Perry if there wasn't something valuable to gain?!

For millennia, jesters have been entertaining, joke tellers have been making up new ways to get a laugh, and class clowns have gone on to become famous comedians. In fact, as far as class clowns are concerned, it is pretty true that such kids usually have something lacking in their lives—some stressor/s or situational problem/s—that make goofing off and cutting up their unique and functional way of coping. *Coping* is how one must necessarily deal with suffering, pain, and sadness lest suicide, drug addiction, depression, or other types of mental illness ruin one's life.

> *Life isn't as serious as the mind makes it out to be.* —Eckert Tolle

There are two main reasons why I find value, fulfillment, and meaning joking around, watching comedy, playing practical jokes, reading *The Onion*, etc. One, it feels good; two, it's helpful. These are two important elements of *coping, psychological adjustment*, and *overcoming*.

Firstly, *as if* we need research to inform us that a sense of humor is a positive thing and that laughing, relating, and not taking things too seriously are good for us! But rest assured, it is out there. Indeed, research psychology has shown, for example:

A healthy sense of humor can help you deal with tough times. Humor might seem like a soothing balm or a light diversion. But humor is much more powerful than something that simply lulls us or calms us down.

It's an often-overlooked tool in our arsenal in the battle to maintain good health. When we are barraged with economic, social, political, and health problems, it's wise to turn to a not-so-obvious way to protect ourselves. The myriad health benefits of humor and laughter are wide-reaching.

During moments of levity, while it seems like you're simply laughing at a friend's joke or a comedian's monologue, you're actually improving your health. By tickling your funny bone, clinical evidence shows you are not only being entertained, but enhancing your physical, psychological, and social well-being.

A man I suppose I guessed was pretty humorless, Washington Irving (you know, Ichabod Crane, the headless horseman, and such) believed, "Honest good humor is the oil and wine of a merry meeting, and there is no jovial companionship equal to that where the jokes are rather small and laughter abundant." I've even read a book about John Adams where it was noted that he would, when he was not fretting or pontificating or promulgating, would have a little fun now and then. His relationship with his wife was, at times, fond and a bit lighthearted. He was no *Thomas Jefferson*, but he was very amiable to those who knew him well. And hey, if it weren't for Jefferson trying to appear so cultured and dignified, we wouldn't find jokes about him *having children with his slave girl*, Sally Hemmings, all that funny. Thanks, T.J.!

> *An onion can make people cry, but there has never been a vegetable invented to make them laugh.* —Will Rogers

My late father was notoriously jocular—it's one of the two reasons folks loved him. And my stepdad was almost always lighthearted. The one joke I recall fondly was when I was staying out in San Diego recovering from a surgery—I used to be a female—*kidding* transgender friends, relax. Anyway, when I would wake up, I would see him—in his robe (like in *just* a robe which wasn't very funny), and he would ask, "Did you sleep well?" I would reply, "Yes," and without fail, his response would be, "You didn't make any mistakes?" Get it? Yah, it wasn't that funny. But to all who knew him, Stanley was, well, *Stanley*. He did tend to cope with challenging emotions by being jokey and lighthearted, and my dad and I are (were) somewhat similar. I definitely connected with my father through humor, and frankly, my mom has a great sense of humor, too—when she is not taking life *entirely too seriously*, as she now does. More on the "coping aspects" of humor in a future paragraph...

Zach Braff of *Scrubs* noted that, "If you can't laugh at yourself, life is going to seem a whole lot longer than you'd like." The deadpan humor he wrote into the script for *Garden State* was pretty good, too. Any movie that will make you laugh and make you cry is alright by me! That movie definitely gets me, and I always seem to tear up when John Candy appears, all lonely and cold, in the end of *Planes, Trains, and Automobiles*. For some reason, my friend and I thought that *The Three Amigos!* was the funniest movie ever written when we were late adolescents. I *still* can't watch Joe Mantegna on the stupendously serious show, *Criminal Minds,* without thinking of his *The Simpsons* role as the Mafioso, or the big Hollywood producer Harry Flugelman in *The Three Amigos! (IT'LL BE A COLD DAY IN HELL BEFORE HARRY FLUGELMAN LETS AN ACTOR TELL HIM WHAT TO DO!)*

My wife and I like to watch *The Office, Brooklyn 99, Funny You Should Ask, Comedians in Cars Getting Coffee, Parks and Recreation,* stand-up comedy, and all kinds of movies. We banter with each other, and frankly, I am responsible for bringing a lot of the humor into the relationship. It's good! It creates connection; it lightens one up; it is a serotonin rush (the neurotransmitter in the brain that is responsible for feeling good. They haven't been making comedies, and comedians haven't been performing for what, *a century?,* for nothing! No, it's impossible to watch Steve Carrell's portrayal of the virgin in *The 40-Year-Old Virgin*, or in *The Office*, without seeing my mood improve. It's like magic. *Humor is akin to magic*, I have to say.

I like Eddie Murphy and Norm McDonald and Anjelah Johnson, but I love Ricky Gervais—the comedian who does stand up, created *The Office*, and who has a pretty good show now called *After Life*. He isn't funny like slapstick or fart jokes; he is extremely incisive, witty and insightful. He believes that, "If you can find humor in life, you're bulletproof." He does not pull punches for women, gays, celebrities, fools—even *God*. A few of my favorites of his are: "Just because you're offended, doesn't mean you're right," and, "Remember, when you are dead, you do not know you are dead. It is only painful for others. The same applies when you are stupid." *Ceaselessly jovial*, the man said at an awards show once, "It's a privilege to be in such a great category of people and all that. . . I don't believe in God, so I'd like to thank dogs. Dogs have given me everything." Now that just hits me right *there*.

Secondly, the part about being helpful is that humor is a way to cope with what is bothering us. "Laughter is a very underrated tool for healing," noted Bronnie Ware. And

Antonia Novello said, "I survived many times in my life by learning to laugh at myself."

Humor has worked for Jews for (I would guess) 5,000 years. I say that a bit tongue-in-cheek, but I think it is part of the culture to communicate verbally—and often!—and share what is in one's heart. If one is feeling good, Jews tend to share that; if it's bad, well, Jews tend to *really* share that! It's probably no surprise that among great 20th century comedians, a disproportionate number of Jews are represented: Jerry Seinfeld, Jackie Mason, the Three Stooges, Rita Rudner, Carl Reiner, Woody Allen, Mel Brooks, George Burns, Groucho Marx, Joan Rivers, Jon Stewart, my main man Larry David, and half of Bill Maher (he's half Catholic). The venerable G. K. Chesterton said, "It is the test of a good religion whether you can joke about it."

A lot of bad stuff has happened to Jews, and it's just not our style to be silent about it. It's *helpful* to express oneself when one is feeling down, anxious, frustrated, etc. Charles Bukowski said, "Some people never go crazy. What truly horrible lives they must lead." It's sometimes either joke or go crazy. Hey, it beats committing suicide, murder, or mass murder. That might sound crude, but clearly, folks who do any of those things are using violence to cope with negative feelings, and *clearly*, there are better ways! A Yiddish proverb goes, "If God lived on earth, all his windows would be broken."

J. J. Proctor points out that, "There are things of deadly earnest that can only be safely mentioned under cover of a joke." Gervais is spot-on when he said, "If you can't joke about the most horrendous things in the world, what's the point of jokes? What's the point in having humor? Humor is to get us over terrible things." Take, for example, "Jokes are better than war. Even the most aggressive jokes are better than the least aggressive wars. Even the longest jokes are better than the shortest wars" (George Mikes). And another George—*Orwell* this time—advised, "A dirty joke is not, of course, a serious attack upon morality, but it is a sort of mental rebellion, a momentary wish that things were otherwise."

> *Never put off till tomorrow what may be done day after tomorrow just as well.* —Mark Twain

This world is often not a fun place, and it can be very disturbing—perhaps especially to the intelligent and sensitive among us. I sometimes feel like the ignorant and the dumb kind of go about their business with a little less pique than those who are artsy like comedians, authors, social critics, etc. *Me*! Author of *The Subtle Art of Not Giving a F#ck*, Mark Manson, notes that:

> Human minds are meaning machines. When something good happens to us, we demand to know why. When something bad happens to us, we also demand to know why. The better or worse the thing that happened, the more powerful the instinct to deduce the reason and cause. The problem is that many of the most impactful events in human history can happen for no apparent reason. This drives the human mind bananas.

Point being, one has to really *stretch* to believe that this world was made just for human beings. It sometimes seems like there is too much wrong—too much bullshit and absurdity and such—to have been artfully designed by a loving god. Maybe I'm missing something.

Incidentally, check out this review of Manson's book on GoodReads.com:

> Whenever a young white dude claims to hold some kind of universal truth, he's usually just talking about himself. And when he's not talking about himself or his sexual exploits, he's mansplaining Eastern philosophy and reminding us that the key to happiness is the acceptance of our own death, which is the only thing I'm thinking about after finishing this book.

Ouch! You can see why it's so hard for people to get along with each other when you read that! But hey, if it's true, it's true. I'm not saying it is, but if Manson can't laugh off a tough review or get stoic about it and deal, then he probably shouldn't have written a self-help book with the word *fuck* in the title.

> *A day without sunshine is like, you know, night.* —Steve Martin

But the world is indeed a screwy place—and America is as screwy *or screwier* than the rest of it. Humor can take the edge off; bring people together. That is very helpful. Take Chris Rock's joke, "If you're black, you got to look at America a little bit different. You got to look at America like the uncle who paid for you to go to college but molested you." I can even see his huge, squinty-eyed grin right now...

Alas, humor seems to be under a lot of pressure lately. When comedy marvel Chevy Chase used to say in the 1970s—completely straight-faced—to his co-anchor on the *SNL* news update, "Jane, you ignorant slut!" it got a laugh. You just kinda *knew* it was nothing to take too seriously; the gag was, you know, *wow, what a way to start the news*; it was brash and outlandish. That was perhaps a bridge too far, but if you ask politicians, priests, and media personalities if they thought *SNL* went too far, they would certainly agree (they tended to get lambasted from 11:30 to 1:00 on Saturdays. So that was a bit much.

Lenny Bruce, Richard Pryor, George Carlin—it was a time of edgy humor and little political correctness. Nowadays, it's all political correctness, all the time. I'm just surprised *The Simpsons* has been on as long as it has, or that Sarah Silverman and Nikki Glaser haven't been burned as witches! Indeed, nowadays, conservatives are fond of "owning the libs" and calling them snowflakes and other more nefarious deeds, and liberals are not laughing at themselves or anything else. I have to agree, as Bill Maher points out, that the political Left "comes up with ideas that sound a lot like a headline from *The Onion* nowadays."

Yes, it is not that funny to have dressed up like a racial minority back in 1983, but to crucify them *now* for it? It's insane. Some folks have no sense of humor about anything—lest they be worried that *joking* about religion is tantamount to *anti-Semitism*, or poking fun of folks who live in a trailer part plays some role in the fact that people are living in a trailer park. And as Dusty Slay says, "If you live in a trailer park, *looks like you made some bad decisions along the way!*" See? It's kinda funny.

I like Gervais's take on how to be funny without being a prick about it: "I think you can make fun of anything except things people can't help. They can't help their race or their sex or their age, so you ridicule their pretension or ego instead. You can ridicule ideas—ideas don't have feelings. You can ridicule an idea that someone holds without hurting them." I think that is very magnanimous of him—he is probably even more willing to give quarter to folks than I am, or someone like Dave Chappelle, since my attitude tends to be, *Ya I don't think making fun of someone who is ugly, to their face, is something that it nice at all, but if they aren't in the room and you're never going to meet them, have a little fun with it; no one gets hurt.*

> *I love mankind ... it's people I can't stand*!! —Charles M. Schulz

But no, joking about someone tripping or being dumb or something is special because, in *reality*, it doesn't *mean* all that much. That's the thing about jokes that non-

188

comedians need to accept: joking about something is not *perpetuating, causing*, or *creating* any real harm. You do have to titrate the potency to not go around stepping on everyone's feelings, but—BUT—as Dennis Miller pointed out twenty years ago, "There's the *joke* world—and then there's the *real* world, and they are not the same."

Chris Rock, Jerry Seinfeld, and, oh yah, *Louis C. K.* would all agree that everyone is taking everything a little too seriously nowadays. One sexist remark or one mistake should not sentence a person to social ostracism forever. We have a lot of serious problems but noting that someone who is fat is, well, *fat*, is not among them. In my opinion. And Bill Maher's. Conservatives think liberals take themselves too seriously, so I personally don't want to feed into that stereotype.

And no, I don't think that liberals need to feel bad about laughing at people, institutions, or the foibles we all possess. *Within reason*. We can all laugh together as *Americans* (remember when Yakov Smirnoff and Johnny Carson and Louie Anderson were the thing; we laughed as Americans). Then after we take a break from reality by finding stuff funny as a unified group, *then* we can get back to trying to provide daycare for all who need it, stopping the destruction of the planet, making the streets safe for African-Americans, and so on. We can do both. *Activism and social justice by day; comedy by night! Pioneering actor and social justice advocate George Takei brilliantly said,* "It's really hard to hate someone for being different when you're too busy laughing together." He doesn't worry much about a bit of spiciness to jokes; he directs his withering gaze at those in power.

> *Our crisis is no longer material; it's existential, it's spiritual. We have so much fucking stuff and so many opportunities that we don't even know what to give a fuck about anymore.* —Mark Manson

Manson also believes:

> Everything worthwhile in life is won through surmounting the associated negative experience. Any attempt to escape the negative, to avoid it or quash it or silence it,

only backfires. The avoidance of suffering is a form of suffering. The avoidance of struggle is a struggle. The denial of failure is a failure. Hiding what is shameful is itself a form of shame.

Not bad for an illegitimate son of that dynamo of the 1960s, Charles Manson! *Kidding*.

I really do think that humor is one of the few things that can bring different people together—along with things like music, food, art, and sex. That reminds me of this one date I had ... *Never mind.*

Have you ever been advised to "*chill the hell out*"? I have and you know what? They were often right. I do take myself and everything in the world too seriously sometimes. Also, I'm a bit of a worrier and certainly a perfectionist. It can be tiresome. It's therefore in my best interest to just relax, slow down, take the edge off, and not sweat the small stuff. Humor can definitely play a positive role there. No one likes criticism or to feel like they are not doing it right, but advice to chill out is sometimes very good advice.

Humor is a way of talking about important, uncomfortable things with somewhat greater ease. Woody Harrelson, famous for his portrayal of the dolt on *Cheers!* said, "The only way to get a serious message across is through comedy." Take this bit of commentary on our educational system, our national priorities, etc.:

> *Graduation time in high schools is the moment to extend sincere congratulations to that elite 49 percent of American students who made it through the system. You all worked very hard for your diplomas, and it's just too bad that most of you won't be able to read them.* —A. Whitney Brown

It's just much easier to start that conversation by creating some mirth; it makes the bitter pill go down easier. This is the formula that has been used with great success by Alan King all the way through to Stephen Colbert. Jimmy Kimmel, Sarah Silverman, Dave Chappelle, Erin Jackson,

Trevor Noah, John Oliver, Kathleen Madigan, George Carlin, Lorne Michaels, Richard Pryor, Lucille Ball, Jim Gaffigan, and Bill Cosby prior to learning what a damn creep he is—they all specialize in showing us all a mirror that we probably need to see. Their incisive wit, self-effacement, and curious perspectives all enlighten the rest of us who are better at eating popcorn and farting than getting up in front of people and making them laugh.

Have you ever seen a "roast"? How about the White House Correspondent's Dinner? *Saturday Night Live*? What do they all have in common? It is more than just three weirdos accidentally hitting each other on the head with boards like *The Three Stooges* did; the point of those efforts is to laugh, yes, but more importantly, to make a point. To share the truth with an audience of co-conspirators. To discuss wisdom without actually using the word *wisdom*. This benefits us because of serotonin and all that, but it really helps us as a society—and God knows we need help!

Comedy can point out things that we all feel—that we share—and that brings us together, and it also highlights the bullshittery we tend to become inured to. For instance, "For a list of all the ways technology has failed to improve the quality of life, please press three," joked Alice Kahn. That's brilliant stuff, but it highlights what is weird about society—always has, always will. Carson joked about funny things from the 1970s and 1980s, and it was golden. Bob Hope—that guy was a *marvel* in prior decades. Folks used to get much of their news from *The Daily Show*—Stewart thought that was just preposterous. But it is what it is—it makes all the nonsense much more palatable to have someone skewering these fools for you. As Alessandra Stanley put it:

> All late-night talk-show hosts make jokes about politicians. What distinguishes Jon Stewart from Jay Leno and David Letterman is that the Comedy Central star mocks the entire political process, boring in tightly on the lockstep thinking and complacency of the parties and the media as well as the candidates. More than any other television analysts and commentators, he and his writers put a spotlight on the inanities and bland hypocrisies that

go mostly unnoticed in the average news cycle.

Indeed, the incredibly smart and very watchable Fareed Zakaria points out that, "The U.S. Congress is a national embarrassment, except that no one is embarrassed."

Satire has a lot of power to it. Take Michael Moore, the filmmaker. He makes solid points and does so often with a dose of humor. It makes for a much more interesting movie; who wants to see two hours of Dick Cheney and George Bush being themselves without any joking?? Philosopher Judith Barad points out, "Michael Moore refuses to pass up an opportunity to show us how ridiculous, how awkward, how vain are the people who've successfully sold themselves as all-knowing Great White Fathers who have the gravitas to be trusted absolutely." And Bill Maher quipped, "If you're living hand-to-mouth, and still buying into the con that the big threats to America are socialized medicine, Mexican immigrants and tax increases, then you're not being kept down by the rich. You're being kept down by *you*."

Take your work seriously but yourself lightly. —C. W. Metcalf

So in sum, laughing feels good, brings people together, lowers tensions, helps your brain, and can point out personal foibles and societal outrages in a new light. It's about the best thing humans have got (well, I sometimes feel my dogs have a bit of an ability to recognize something that is a bit funny). Let's not take joking too seriously because the world is so damned serious that we're shooting ourselves in the foot if we sweat the small stuff. If you're gay, you've got to deal with being gay in society, and stopping for a sec to laugh about it is only helpful; if you're black, you've got some automatic problems, and humor is bound to be part of your solution. If you're uneducated, white, and Southern—well, the rest of us are laughing *with* you, not *at* you, I assure you. *It's cool man,* PUT THE GUN DOWN!!

I will end with a snappy little quote from a girl who, to the everlasting shame of the world, had the humor sucked right out of her by evil. If *The Diary of Anne Frank* doesn't make a reader come to believe that human beings are horribly fallible creatures *but do have a bright side*—including possessing some very useful mechanisms for coping with sorrow, loss, and misfortune—then they might have, like Trump with his infamous/horrible "Bible photo-op stunt," been inadvertently holding the *Diary* upside down the whole time!

> I have often been downcast, but never in despair; I regard our hiding as a dangerous adventure, romantic and interesting at the same time. In my diary, I treat all the privations as amusing. I have made up my mind now to lead a different life from other girls and, later on, different from ordinary housewives. My start has been so very full of interest, and that is the sole reason why I have to laugh at the humorous side of the most dangerous moments.

Now, more quotes to make you think—and to laugh!

"People who cannot recognize a palpable absurdity are very much in the way of civilization." —Agnes Repplier

"Anyone without a sense of humor is at the mercy of everyone else." —William E. Rothschild

"I like Ted Cruz more than most of my other colleagues like Ted Cruz. And I hate Ted Cruz." —Al Franken

"He who laughs, lasts." —Anonymous

"Analyzing humor is like dissecting a frog. Few people are interested, and the frog dies of it." —E. B. White

"We do not take humor seriously enough." —Konrad Lorenz

"What else can so enjoyably exercise the heart and boost the mood? What else can serve so well as both a social signal and a conversational lubricant? What else can bond parents to children, siblings to one another, and teach powerful lessons about staying alive in a tooth-and-claw world? Laughter may seem like little more than evolution's whoopee cushion, but if scientists studying it are right, we owe it an awful lot of thanks for some surprisingly serious things." —Jeffrey Kluger

"Laughter without a tinge of philosophy is but a sneeze of humor. Genuine humor is replete with wisdom." —Mark Twain

"Is it to be understood that the principles of the Declaration of Independence bear no relation to half of the human race?" —Harriet Martineau

"My friend Larry's in jail now. He got twenty-five years for something he didn't do—he didn't run fast enough." —Damon Wayans

"Like a welcome summer rain, humor may suddenly cleanse and cool the earth, the air and you." —Langston Hughes

"Be nice to people on your way up because you'll meet them on the way down." —Wilson Mizner

"Trump may not feel he is a racist, but racists think he is a racist." —April Ryan

"The majority of our citizens, of every ideological persuasion, share the same disquieting suspicion: that we are powerless to fix our broken institutions. For some, religion remains a source of salvation. Others place their trust in the bluster of demagogues, or simply choose to live in a fog of frantic material and athletic distraction. The rest of us—the Troubled but Tame Majority, let's say—chose to embrace Jon

Stewart as our spirit guide. Because he was the one public figure capable of articulating the depth of our dysfunction without totally bumming us out. He converted our despair, instead, into laughter. But something more insidious was happening in the process. We were learning to see politics and media as a joke." —Steve Almond

"Consider the case of Stephen Crawford, former co-president of Morgan Stanley, who was rewarded for three months of presiding over the company's decline with a $32 million pay-off. That's $32 million for screwing up, or, if we generously assume he put in ten hours a day at this task, about $30,000 per hour." —Barbara Ehrenreich

"Millionaires are so *last millennium*. The new Forbes 400 list of richest Americans is billionaires only." —Holly Sklar

"I saw a personal ad that looked interesting. It said she loved long walks, running on the beach, going to parks. As it turns out, she was a German Shepherd." —David Corrado

"A person reveals his character by nothing so clearly as the joke he resents." —G. C. Lichtenberg

"A lot of things go on when you're a kid that you don't figure out until you're an adult.

Like, I think my kindergarten teacher had a drinking problem, because naptime was every day from 9:00 to 2:30." —Janine DiTullio

"I always give homeless people money, and my friends yell at me, 'He's only going to buy more alcohol and cigarettes.' And I'm thinking, 'Oh, like I wasn't?'" —Kathleen Madigan

"I don't wanna die tomorrow knowing that I could have had a piece of chocolate cake tonight." —Gabriel Iglesias

"At the hands of the best comics, laughter hence acquires a moral purpose, jokes become attempts to cajole others into reforming their character and habits. Jokes are a way of sketching a political ideal, of creating a more equitable and saner world. Wherever there is inequity or delusion, space opens up for humor-clad criticisms." —Alain de Botton

"My husband and I have never considered divorce. Murder sometimes, but never divorce." —Joyce Brothers

"In America any boy may become President, and I suppose it's just one of the risks he takes." —Adlai Stevenson

"Some of the most politically incorrect people on the planet, such as David Letterman and Jay Leno, are staples of late-night TV. Enjoying the temporary immunity of the court jester, their job is to good-naturedly butcher everybody's sacred cows. But you'd better not repeat any of their jokes on the job or in the classroom, in case someone takes 'offense' today at something millions of viewers laughed at yesterday." — Lou Marinoff

"I look at husbands the same way I look at tattoos. I want one but I can't decide what I want and I don't want to be stuck with one I'm just going to grow to hate and have to have surgically removed later." —Margaret Cho

"Kids? It's like living with homeless people. They're cute but they just chase you around all day long going, 'Can I have a dollar? I'm missing a shoe! I need a ride!" —Kathleen Madigan

Jason Merchey is the founder of an approach to fulfillment, meaning, and happiness—coping as well—called Values of the Wise™ Since 2004, the site has centered around quotations about values and virtues, wisdom and ethics. There are many free tools, and there are never any advertisements. The goal is to fuse classical values with progressive thinking, and to bring great thinking to life. Ideally, one can learn to make wisdom their greatest strength. Wisdom is the heart of the matter, Jason believes; In fact, his most recent book (2022) is entitled *Wisdom: A Very Valuable Virtue That Cannot Be Bought* (available on his website, and wherever books are sold online). The book has garnered some critical success and, Jason *hopes*, is making an impact on an ailing America. Stoicism, existentialism, Humanism, and sexism (*kidding!*) are certainly important themes in the book, as successful coping (individually as well as societally) is a goal Jason tends to think about, write about, and aspire to. He obtained a master's degree in psychology and graduated from university with highest honors. Jason lives in western North

Carolina with his wife and dog. His website is www.ValuesoftheWise.com

Summary Guide

1. TO SUFFER IS TO LIVE.

- There are countless theoretical approaches to understanding the universal problem of suffering. We start with the Buddhist conception, which sees pain as an inevitable and natural part of life, which is transient and always changing. Therefore if we attach to what is impermeant, we will suffer when it changes.
- The parable of the farmer and the Buddha shows that our biggest problem is that we believe we should have no problems.
- In these views, suffering occurs because, paradoxically, we think we should not be suffering!
- Pain is unavoidable, but suffering is optional. Suffering is pain plus our grasping, resistance, attachment or identification. Thus we can greatly

reduce our suffering by changing how we deal with pain.

- The serenity prayer teaches us that we need the wisdom to discern between what is in our power to control (our mental reaction to pain) and what isn't (the pain itself).

- According to Viktor Frankl, in the brief moment after pain, we have a gap where we can pause and decide what response we would like to have. We may evolve mechanisms to respond automatically, but we also have the power to choose our response if we are conscious.

- Cognitive behavioral psychologists recognize a similar principle, and explain how our minds can trap us in suffering. We experience pain and then immediately create a thought about it. This thought creates our feelings and a physiological reaction, for example, stress and tension in the body. In time, these feelings spiral out of control and manifest as behaviors that reinforce our original thoughts.

2. THE CAUSES OF SUFFERING

- In the Buddhist tradition, the four noble truths explain what suffering is, its cause, and how to deal with it. The first truth is that suffering exists and is unavoidable, and the second is that the cause of suffering is our desire, craving or attachment. The third is that suffering can be released if we renounce this attachment, and the fourth truth is that we practice this way of being by following the eight-fold path.

- When we are attached to one outcome or another, the Buddhists claim we cause suffering. It is our perspective, preference, narrative, and expectation about what should be that causes our unhappiness. In life, everything is transient, though, and always changing.

- In the parable of the two monks, we see that resistance is also a form of grasping, and allows us to "carry" suffering with us long after the initial moment has passed.

- In this philosophy, we cannot achieve happiness by trying to remove suffering from life, but rather by changing our attitude to it.

- We can use the four noble truths as a starting point for reducing suffering in our own lives, or rather, learn to suffer better. To do so, we have to understand our own tendency to identify with, cling, resist or tell stories about reality and learn to simply appreciate reality for what it is: neutral and impermanent.

3. WHAT DO WE DO WITH SUFFERING, THEN?

- Once we can properly identify suffering for what it is and become aware of it in ourselves, we can begin to manage it better.
- Suffering takes all different forms for each of us, but according to the four noble truths, there is a way to ease and reduce our suffering, by letting go of attachment.
- One way to do this is to practice distinguishing between pain and suffering, first and second darts, and facts or opinions. When you feel upset, slow down and tease apart the situation until

you see it as clearly and objectively as possible.

- Try to avoid extremes and black-and-white, all-or-nothing thinking. Watch out for clues to cognitive distortions and bias like absolute terms, catastrophizing and generalization, and instead look for a balanced path down the middle of extremes. We can achieve this merely by changing our language and how we frame things.

- Counterintuitively, we reduce feelings of suffering by being willing to "sit with" and acknowledge all our feelings, without trying to escape them. We can learn to stay in the present and be aware of how we feel right now, instead of letting our minds get carried away with thoughts of the past or future. One way to keep in the present is to ground in the senses.

- Finally, take care with what you consume, information-wise, since suffering is often a question of overwhelm, or being looped into people's stories and interpretations. Pay close attention to the media you take in, its effect on you, and how these distractions may be helping you avoid your feelings in the present.

4. STOICISM'S APPROACH TO BEAT SUFFERING

- The Stoics, like the Buddhists, understood that pain is just a part of life, and taught that we need to retain quiet, dignified serenity in the face of adversity, focusing on what we can control, while accepting what we can't. One way to practice the Stoic philosophy is to carefully consider your zone of control or, as Byron Katie suggests, identify what is your business, the other person's business, and God's business.
- Another technique is to use negative visualization to develop gratitude for everything you already have. By imagining that things could be a lot worse, you re-calibrate your expectations and focus more with appreciation on the present. We also desensitize ourselves to discomfort and learn that we can, in fact, endure it.

- One way to empower ourselves in the face of life's pain is to take action. Action grounds us. We can always seek to elevate the situation we find ourselves in, draw on our strengths, and work with what we have. We can choose to build, create and solve problems. We can do this if we stop wasting energy on those things we have no hope of changing.

- Finally, we can become cognizant of the fact that resistance and struggle come with a cost, and inevitably cause us to suffer, all while doing nothing to improve our lives. Though our brains may be primed for a certain kind of negativity, we can always choose to create meaning, do a good deed or take productive action to improve things.

5. FRANKL'S APPROACH TO SUFFERING

- Viktor Frankl experienced extreme hardship and suffering and, from this, developed his own theory about how many searches for and creates his own meaning. Frankl's experiences taught him that suffering pushes human beings to find meaning and purpose in their lives. To survive, in other words, is to find meaning in one's suffering.

- Frankl believed that struggle with suffering is an opportunity to seek and create something deeper and more meaningful, identify values and principles, and even deepen one's spiritual understanding.
- Instead of searching for meaning externally, we have to look at our own unique strengths and calling in life, and hear what life demands from us, rather than making demands of it. This means that we need to take concrete action.
- Frankl thought that there were 3 ways to find meaning in life: We can work or create something of value, we can truly encounter another human being, or we can make meaning out of our suffering.
- One way to do this is to fine-tune your own unique purpose. Suffering can force us to look closely at what really matters to us most in life, but knowing our values also allows us to suffer better.

- Another remedy for suffering, according to Frankl, is to have compassion, and to be guided by love. Frankl sees love as mankind's highest possibility, and when we choose kindness and empathy, we can take any form of suffering and redeem it.

6. SUFFER BETTER, SUFFER LESS

- The fourth noble truth encourages us to follow the eight-fold path, i.e. we need to understand suffering but also take concrete *action* towards our intended life every day. We can use proven and effective tools to help us suffer better, and suffer less.
- Firstly, we can learn the power of reframing so that we investigate the "rules" we have for deciding what counts as pain or suffering in the first place. Much suffering disappears when we take our own assumptions and interpretations out of the picture.
- Emotions are fleeting and always changing. When we understand this, we

don't cling to one emotion or reject another. It's useful to learn to accept, embrace and name emotions for what they are, so they can flow.

- A third tip is to understand that effort and difficulty don't always signal pain, and rather than being something to avoid, it can be enriching. Get into the habit of asking whether you are really suffering or whether you are just experiencing the inevitable discomfort of change and growth.

- Realize that sometimes, pain and suffering may be a sign that something needs to change. Pain can be a wake-up call if we heed its message honestly. Not all pain has to be stoically endured. Be frank with yourself about the cause of pain in your life, and what its message is.

- Finally, understand that even raw, blind pain such as the pain experienced by endurance pro-athletes is not the end of the world. Those who fare best tend to have an attitude of "no option." They distract themselves when it comes to discomfort and don't allow themselves to indulge in thoughts of giving up.

- Stay present. It's something we hear frequently, but what does it mean? Simply put, we are more often caught in the past or looking forward to the future. When we are caught in the past, we are affected by things and events that we have no control over. When we are looking forward to the future (excessively, of course), we are also affected by that which we have no control over.

- Author Eckhart Tolle has great insight into the problem of fixating on the past or future; he once said, "All negativity is caused by an accumulation of psychological time and denial of the present. Unease, anxiety, tension, stress, worry—all forms of fear—are caused by too much *future* and not enough presence. Guilt, regret, resentment, grievances, sadness, bitterness, and all forms of non-forgiveness are caused by too much *past*, and not enough presence."

215

- To let go of the past is to forgive, excuse, and allow for errors. We can learn from the past, and we don't have to experience things in vain. To stop fixating on the future is to accept uncertainty and a certain amount of randomness. We cannot control very much in our lives, and all we can control is our actions and reactions.
- Staying in the present is of course easier said than done, but the practice of meditation is a useful blueprint. It is important to clear your mind and simply lose yourself in a thought, feeling, or sensation. Preoccupation is the worst of sins here, and it can only be defeated with time and practice—and the knowledge that the past does not matter anymore and the future is out of our control.

Ingram Content Group UK Ltd.
Milton Keynes UK
UKHW011047310323
419466UK00003B/90